Co

BIRDS

of

Southwestern British Columbia

Lower Mainland & Vancouver Island

Violet-green Swallow

J. Duane Sept

Calypso Publishing

First edition

Front Cover Photo: Marsh wren by J. Duane Sept.
Back Cover Photos: Northern pintail drake, sandhill crane and rufous hummingbird by J. Duane Sept.

Printed and bound in China.

Library and Archives Canada Cataloguing in Publication

Sept, J. Duane, 1950-, author
Common birds of southwestern British Columbia : Lower Mainland and Vancouver Island / J. Duane Sept.

Includes bibliographical references and index.
ISBN 978-0-9739819-9-5 (paperback)

1. Birds--British Columbia--Vancouver Island--Identification. 2. Birds--British Columbia--Lower Mainland--Identification. I. Title.

QL685.5.B7S467 2016 598.09711'3 C2015-904564-9

Published by:
Calypso Publishing
P.O. Box 1141
Sechelt, BC Canada
V0N 3A0

Website: http://www.calypso-publishing.com

Table of Contents

Quick Photo Guide to the Bird Groups

Swans p. 13

Ducks & Geese p. 13

Grouse p. 26

Loons p. 29

Grebes p. 29

Cormorants p. 31

Herons & Bitterns p. 32

Hawks & Eagles p. 34

Rails & Cranes p. 40

Shorebirds p. 42

Diving Seabirds p. 51

Gulls & Terns p. 51

Welcome to Birding

The pursuit of observing birds has become one of the fastest growing recreational activities in North America, from a casual and occasional pastime to an intense passion. Birding can be enjoyed in urban and rural settings and at any time of year—spring, summer, fall and winter. Some birders have life lists and many participate in Christmas bird counts as well as breeding bird surveys. Still others plan their vacations around good birding locations.

The sights and sounds of our winged wonders bring pleasure to all, young and old, and a great deal of interesting information has been discovered about our birds and their behaviors. This book will invite all birders to understand and appreciate the magnificent free-fliers of the Pacific Northwest.

How to Use This Book

The birds in this book are arranged in order of evolutionary sequence, the method that is used in most bird references. This order is quickly learned and makes it easier for the novice to find specific groups of birds, such as ducks, in other books about birds.

The quick photo guide on p. 4-5 will aid you in finding the main bird groups and narrowing your search.

Parts of a Bird

Song sparrow.

Species Information and Identifying Features

Color photographs, descriptions and concise information are included for each bird.

NAME The current accepted common name and scientific or Latin name.

Description The most distinguishing physical features, to aid in identification.

Size Dimensions for large individuals of the species.

Nesting Nest site and materials, along with usual number and color of eggs.

Habitat Type of area where the species lives, sometimes with added information if there are seasonal habitats.

Notes Natural history notes on each species, offering interesting information on behavior, populations or special characteristics.

Similar Species Distinguishing features of similar birds.

Tips and Techniques for Better Birding

Birdsong

Although birding can be conducted at any time of the day, the best time to observe many species, during the breeding season, is early morning while the males are singing. Listen for birdsong, since many species have distinctive calls and songs. It is possible to identify many species by voice before you can see them. This is especially true during the spring and summer, and, for some species, during the entire year.

Calling Birds

One technique that often brings birds closer, so that you can get a better view, is to call them. Try making a repeated "swishing" sound. Other calls such as *pishh* and *Sip! Sip! Sip*! can also be effective, as well as noises made by squeaking the back of the hand in a sort of "kissing" sound. This technique should not be used excessively in one area, as it can stress breeding birds.

Some smaller bird species are sometimes affectionately referred to as "little brown jobs" (LBJs) if they cannot be identified. Sandpipers, which can also be difficult to identify, are sometimes referred to as "peeps."

Choosing Equipment

Binoculars

Binoculars are an excellent tool for observing all birds. They do not have to be large or heavy—they should be powerful enough to magnify the subject sufficiently but should not be too difficult to hold steady. Binoculars are rated by both their magnification and light-gathering capacity. A pair of binoculars with a rating of 7 x 40 can magnify the subject 7 times or 700%. If you are looking for your first pair of binoculars, I recommend that you choose a pair with a wide range of vision. This will aid you greatly in getting the bird in view, a skill that takes practice to learn. A pair of binoculars with 10 power, for example, may have too narrow a field of vision for beginning birders.

The second number in the designation—40, in the 7 x 40 binoculars—is the diameter of the objective lens (in millimeters) where the light enters. The larger this number, the more light is available for viewing in low-light situations, including dusk and dawn. A good beginning pair of binoculars for birding is 7 x 35 or 7 x 40. Higher magnifications and light-gathering properties are excellent for a second pair, once you have experience at finding the birds in your binoculars. Low-light conditions may not apply at the time of day when you are observing birds.

Be sure to talk to others about the advantages and disadvantages of their binoculars. A good way to do this is to join an outdoor club. The more you can try out various binoculars in the field, the more informed choice you will be.

Spotting Scopes

Many serious birding enthusiasts use spotting scopes, because they make it possible to see more details of a bird at greater distances. A tripod or car window can be used to steady this excellent tool. Magnification begins at approximately 20 times. Excellent zoom optics are available, with which you can zero in on your subject. Spotting scopes are more costly than many binoculars, depending upon quality, magnification capability and brand.

Virtual Birding Sites

Several websites are available to help birders find and observe birds. The following sites were available at the time this book was written (August 2015).

The Bird Guide: Your guide to birds and birding in the Pacific Northwest
http://thebirdguide.com/

eBird Canada (Recent sightings by province)
http://ebird.ca/

Virtual Birder (Rare Bird Alerts)
http://www.virtualbirder.com/vbirder/realbirds/index.html

Birding in BC
http://birding.bc.ca/

North American Bird Sounds
http://www.naturesongs.com/birds.html

Attracting Birds to Your Home

Food

Giving birds a nutritious meal is an excellent way to bring them close to your home and garden and to experience the wonders of nature. Many people think that if ducks or other birds eat bread or crackers, it must be OK to give it to them. But no birds should be fed bread, crackers, chips or similar foods meant for people. These items have no nutritional value for birds, so they actually rob the birds of the nourishment they need to migrate or to survive the winter. A variety of wild bird seed is available at specialty stores.

It is very gratifying to attract birds year-round and observe them on a regular basis. Select foods that are appropriate for the species you wish to attract. Place your feeder at a site where you can observe the birds but not startle them while they feed. Elevate the feeding area so that the birds can watch for predators, including domestic cats, and place it away from cover such as trees, to prevent cats from capturing "your" birds. At times, hawks and owls may also frequent a feeder, to find an easy meal.

Birdhouses

Many species of birds, including wrens, swallows and tree-nesting ducks, will readily accept an appropriate man-made birdhouse as a place to raise a family. See the references listed on p. 90 for tips on building birdhouses. Feeders and birdhouses are also available commercially.

Gardening to Attract Birds

Several trees, shrubs, herbs and other native plants attract many species of birds and satisfy some of their seasonal needs. Plants can provide seeds, berries and nectar, as well as nesting sites and/or materials.

In the Pacific Northwest, several native wildflowers, such as columbine (*Aquilegia* spp.) and penstemon (*Penstemon* spp.), are favorites of hummingbirds. Native plants that attract seed- and fruit-eating birds include maple (*Acer* spp.), arbutus (*Arbutus menziesii*), birch (*Betula* spp.), dogwood (*Cornus* spp.), hawthorn (*Crataegus* spp.), chokecherry (*Prunus virginiana*), crabapple (*Pyrus* spp.) and oak (*Quercus* spp.). In addition, several non-native plants that attract birds are available at nurseries.

However, please note that some plants, such as bracted honeysuckle (*Lonicera involucrata*), produce berries that are poisonous to humans, and are best avoided if they would be within reach of small children.

Where to Find Birds in Southwestern British Columbia

There are many excellent locations to discover birds in the Lower Mainland and on Vancouver Island. In this part of the world you may see birds almost anywhere, but these sites present particularly good opportunities to observe a wide variety of species. Most of them offer excellent bird viewing all year round.

Lower Mainland

Burnaby
Burnaby Lake Regional Park, Burnaby

Delta
George C. Reifel Migratory Bird Sanctuary, Delta
Boundary Bay Dyke Trail, Delta (Foot access 64th, 72nd or 104th Street)

Hope
Manning Provincial Park, Hope

Richmond
Iona Beach Regional Park, Richmond

Surrey
Blackie Spit, Crescent Beach, Surrey

Tsawwassen
Centennial Beach, Boundary Bay Regional Park, Tsawwassen
BC Ferries Terminal and Jetty, Tsawwassen

Vancouver
Stanley Park, Vancouver
Jericho Beach Park, Vancouver
John Hendry Park (Trout Lake), Vancouver

West Vancouver
Ambleside Park, West Vancouver

Vancouver Island

Victoria Area
Beacon Hill Park, Victoria
Esquimalt Lagoon, Colwood
Cattle Point, Victoria
Swan Lake, Victoria
Goldstream Provincial Park, Victoria

Nanaimo Area
Neck Point (turn East on Hammond Bay Road), Nanaimo
Hemer Provincial Park, Nanaimo
Buttertubs Marsh Park, Nanaimo

Parksville–Qualicum Beach Area
Englishman River Estuary, Parksville
Rathtrevor Beach Provincial Park, Parksville (brant from February to April)
Deep Bay Spit

Four Timing Tips for Best Viewing

- Spring and fall are the best seasons to observe a greater number of bird species.
- For most species, bird song is especially exuberant during the morning hours in spring and summer.
- Winter is a prime time to see the many raptors that winter in this area.
- The best time to view birds at the seashore, especially during shorebird migration, is near the peak of a rising tide.

Area Map

Area covered in this guide.

Note

(I) indicates bird is an introduced species

Trumpeter Swan *Cygnus buccinator*

Description **Adult:** White overall; neck elongated; bill and forehead form a straight ridge; bill black. **Juvenile:** Gray overall; bill pinkish with black tip.
Size Length to 60″ (150 cm).
Nesting **Nest:** At water's edge, or built up in shallow water. **Eggs:** Normally 5–7, pale green.
Habitat Fresh water and salt water shorelines.
Notes The experience of observing trumpeter swans flying close by in a foggy mist is truly memorable. This is an impressive swan and a commonly seen migrant in the Pacific Northwest in early spring, on its way to northern British Columbia and Alaska. As well, many individuals winter along the coast south to Oregon. The trumpeter swan is named for its deep, distinctive, resonant voice, somewhat like the sound of a French horn. It is the largest of all North American waterfowl and requires a stretch of water 20′ (6 m) long to become airborne.
Similar Species: **Tundra swan (*Cygnus columbianus*)** is a similar swan that also migrates through the area while on its way to the Arctic. Its bill has a yellow patch of skin, and its voice resembles the sound produced by reed instruments. **Mute swan (*Cygnus olor*)** is an introduced species from Europe, often seen in urban parks. This species has an orange bill.

Observations: ____________, 20____; ______________________________________

____

Snow Goose *Chen caerulescens*

Description White overall; neck slender, wings with black tips.
Size Length to 28″ (70 cm).
Nesting **Nest:** On a ridge or hummock; in colonies. **Eggs:** Normally 3–5, whitish.
Habitat Various coastal and interior areas on migration.
Notes Fall brings skeins or flocks of snow geese to the coastal regions of the Pacific Northwest. These annual migrations are an impressive sight, accompanied by an equally impressive noisy, excited clamor. Thousands of snow geese stay along the coast at their feeding areas until late March, when they begin migrating to their breeding grounds on Wrangel Island in northeast Siberia. Snows are known to cruise to altitudes as great as 6,000′ (1,800 m) while on migration. There are two color phases of this species: white and blue (rarely observed in the Pacific Northwest). The total population has increased dramatically in recent years.

Observations: ____________, 20____; ______________________________________

____

Brant *Branta bernicla*

Description Black overall; hind end white.
Size Length to 25″ (63 cm).
Nesting **Nest:** On the ground, made of grasses. **Eggs:** Normally 3–5, creamy white.
Habitat Along coastal bays and estuaries.
Notes Migrating along the coast in March and April, this salt water goose makes its way north to breed in the tundra. Its feeding activities are regulated by the movements of the tides. The brant is well known for dining at "salad bars" of sea lettuce and eel-grass. It is an omnivore that also feeds on mollusks, worms and crustaceans. Migrating flocks do not form the "V" shape common in other geese. Instead they fly in undulating lateral strings of birds, seemingly without a leader. Fall migration is faster than spring, with both groups and scattered individuals moving through the area.

Observations: __________, 20____; ______________________________

____

Canada Goose *Branta canadensis*

Description Back and wings brown; head and neck black with a distinctive white chinstrap.
Size Length to 45″ (114 cm).
Nesting **Nest:** On the ground near water, in a tree, up to 102′ (31 m) off the ground, or at the edge of a cliff. Nest is made of sticks, grass and moss, and lined with down. **Eggs:** Normally 4–7, white.
Habitat Fresh water or salt water areas.
Notes The Canada goose is a common year-round resident over much of North America. Its numbers have increased steadily, largely because of the work of biologists and the availability of large new feeding areas such as golf courses. Today their nests can also be found within the boundaries of many cities. Canada geese mate for life and are known to live as long as 30 years. They usually feed on a variety of vegetation, and young geese gain weight rapidly and fledge in 63 days. Their migration is characterized by flying "V" formations.
Similar Species **Cackling goose (*Branta hutchinsii*)** is a very small goose (the same length as the mallard) that closely resembles the Canada goose except that it has a small, short bill and a rounded head.

Observations: __________, 20____; ______________________________

____

Wood Duck *Aix sponsa*

Description **Breeding male:** Head iridescent green with flattened crest; breast reddish brown. **Female:** Much more subdued in color; head with a white eye ring.
Size Length to 18" (45 cm).
Nesting **Nest:** In a large tree cavity or nest box close to water, up to 65' (20 m) off the ground. **Eggs:** Normally 9–14, white to buff.
Habitat Near lakes surrounded by deciduous woodland.
Notes When it comes to color, few birds rival the striking male wood duck, a spectacular species that is named for its habitat of wooded areas. This duck is also well known for its ability to fly through woodlands by twisting and dodging, without losing a beat. When young ducks hatch, they leap to the ground and make their way to the water. In many areas of this species' range, tree cavities are uncommon, so nest boxes are built to attract nesting pairs. These boxes have proven successful in dramatically increasing populations.

Observations: ____________, 20____; ____
____

Green-winged Teal *Anas crecca*

Description Speculum green. **Breeding male:** Gray overall; head cinnamon with an iridescent green ear patch. **Female:** Brown overall.
Size Length to 14.5" (36 cm).
Nesting **Nest:** On the ground, made of grasses, weeds and twigs, and lined with down. **Eggs:** Normally 6–11, cream to buff.
Habitat Fresh water and salt water areas.
Notes This common species, well known for its swift flight, is a small duck, often found in small flocks. It is known to live as long as 16 years, although the average lifespan is probably shorter. Nests are located in woodland areas near wetlands. The male's voice is a distinctive high-pitched whistle, while the female's is reminiscent of the mallard's quack.

Observations: ____________, 20____; ____
____

Mallard *Anas platyrhynchos*

Description Adult: Speculum or wing patch bright blue with white edges; legs and feet bright orange. **Breeding male:** Head iridescent green.

Size Length to 23″ (58 cm).

Nesting Nest: Normally on the ground, made of reeds or grasses, and lined with down. **Eggs:** Normally 7–10, occasionally to 15, olive.

Habitat Marshes, ponds, bogs, lakes and similar situations.

Notes The mallard is likely the most common species of waterfowl in North America and perhaps in the entire north temperate zone. Its presence is often announced by the loud *quack, quack, quack* of the female. These ducks dine on a wide variety of foods, including aquatic vegetation, seeds and aquatic insects, and they are well known, especially by hunters, for their love of grain and corn. The mallard is a familiar sight in urban parks throughout much of North America. It is important not to feed bread to this species or any wild bird, because it has no nutritional value for birds (see p. 9).

Observations: ____________, 20____; ________________________________

Northern Pintail *Anas acuta*

Description Breeding male: Head chocolate brown; body gray; breast white; tail elongated. **Female:** Overall brown; tail pointed.

Size Length to 26″ (65 cm).

Nesting Nest: On the ground, made of grasses and leaves, and lined with down. **Eggs:** Normally 6–10, pale olive.

Habitat Wetlands.

Notes It is reported that more than a million northern pintails migrate along the Pacific coast to the breeding areas of Alaska. Like mallards (see above), these birds migrate in large flocks. In the northern pintail, as in many birds, females are often subtle in coloration while their mates are brightly colored. This difference is believed to aid in the survival of a species. Females normally incubate the eggs, and their subdued coloration helps prevent them from being detected by predators. The bright colors of males, on the other hand, draw attention away from the female and the nest site.

Observations: ____________, 20____; ________________________________

Blue-winged Teal *Anas discors*

Description **Breeding male:** Head bluish gray with white crescent; wing with large blue patch and green speculum. **Female:** Brown overall; wing with large blue patch and green speculum.
Size Length to 16″ (40 cm).
Nesting **Nest:** On the ground in open areas, made of grasses and weeds lining a depression. **Eggs:** Normally 9–13, white to olive.
Habitat Ponds and marshes.
Notes The blue-winged teal is a rapid flyer with expert aviation skills, twisting and turning with fine precision in small groups. This species rarely tips up. It feeds primarily on the water surface and occasionally on the shoreline, eating mainly seeds as well as vegetative portions of aquatic plants. The blue-winged teal migrates north in late spring, and shortens its northern stay even further by returning early in the fall. Ring-necked pheasants (p. 26) have been known occasionally to lay their eggs in the nests of the blue-winged teal.

Observations: ____________, 20____; ______________________________
____

Cinnamon Teal *Anas cyanoptera*

Description **Breeding male:** Overall deep cinnamon red; eyes red; green speculum. **Female:** Overall mottled brown; eyes brown; green speculum.
Size Length to 17″ (43 cm).
Nesting **Nest:** Placed on ground near water. Concealed in areas of sedges, weeds and salt grass. The nest is simply a depression with dead grass and weeds included. **Eggs:** Normally 9–12, white to pale buff.
Habitat Primarily freshwater and shallow alkaline lakes, as well as ponds.
Notes The cinnamon teal is a rather shy duck that prefers smaller lakes and ponds. It breeds in the interior and may be observed elsewhere in southern British Columbia on migration. The striking male's plumage always attracts attention and makes this species easy to identify. Male cinnamon teal are one of the few ducks that remain with the female throughout the summer nesting cycle.

Observations: ____________, 20____; ______________________________
____

Northern Shoveler *Anas clypeata*

Description **Breeding male:** White overall; head iridescent green; body with orange patches on sides; bill large and spoon-shaped. **Female:** Brown overall; bill large and spoon-shaped.
Size Length to 19″ (48 cm).
Nesting **Nest:** On the ground, near water, made of dried grasses and weeds, and lined with down. **Eggs:** Normally 9–12, pale olive.
Habitat Marshes, ponds, bogs, lakes and similar situations.
Notes This common puddle duck is often seen in small groups, during migration to and from the nesting areas. Courtship rituals begin with the male uttering a guttural *konk, konk, konk* while repeatedly craning his neck and raising his head. If the female approves, the two birds swim in circles, one behind the other, with water running through their bills. Eventually the female lays her eggs in a ground nest. During migration, these ducks may be observed in larger numbers feeding together in various wetlands.

Observations: ____________, 20____; ____

____

Gadwall *Anas strepera*

Description **Breeding male:** Gray overall; belly white; rump black; wing patch white. **Female:** Overall a mixture of browns; belly white; wing patch white.
Size Length to 20″ (50 cm).
Nesting **Nest:** On the ground, often near water, made of dried grasses and weeds, and lined with down. **Eggs:** Normally 8–10, white. Some nests contain the eggs of 2 or more females.

Habitat Wetlands.
Notes The gadwall often goes unnoticed because of its dull coloration, but the colors are distinctive upon close examination. The female gadwall is especially impressed with the male's speculum and black color. Gadwalls are dabblers that favor small wetlands as their resorts and breeding areas. Most are year-round residents, but many individuals migrate through the area on their way to northern breeding areas. Some long-distance migrants have been known to travel as far as 1,500 miles (2,500 km) to reach their southern destination.

Observations: ____________, 20____; ____

____

Eurasian Wigeon *Anas penelope*

Description **Breeding male:** Gray overall; head reddish brown with a cream-colored forehead. **Female:** Reddish overall.
Size Length to 20″ (50 cm).
Nesting **Nest:** On the ground, usually near water. Nest materials include dried grasses; nest is lined with down. **Eggs:** Normally 8–9, whitish.
Habitat Fresh water and salt water areas.
Notes Eurasian wigeons are often observed individually or in small numbers, mixed in with large flocks of the American wigeon (see below). In fact, these visitors are one of the treasures that birders look for among American wigeon. A winter migrant that originated in Siberia and western Alaska, the Eurasian wigeon is rarely seen here during the summer months. Males are seen more often than females, because females are very similar to female American wigeons and often go unnoticed.

Observations: ____________, 20____; ____
____

American Wigeon *Anas americana*

Description **Breeding male**: Gray head with a white cap and green ear patch. **Female:** Brown overall; head gray; belly white. **Adult:** White wing patch.
Size Length to 19″ (48 cm).
Nesting **Nest:** On the ground, made of dried grasses and weeds, and lined with down. **Eggs:** Normally 8–11, whitish.
Habitat Areas near fresh water and salt water.
Notes The American wigeon, a common year-round resident of the coast, feeds primarily on vegetation, especially pond weeds, grasses, algae and sedges. Large flocks are often found wintering in areas that have big grassy areas, such as golf courses. American wigeons are also known to help themselves to the food items accidentally dropped by diving water birds, including the canvasback (p. 20) and American coot (p. 41). The American wigeon was once called the baldpate because of the white or "bald" spot on the head.

Observations: ____________, 20____; ____
____

Canvasback *Aythya valisineria*

Description **Male:** Body white; head red; forehead slopes smoothly into the long bill. **Female:** Body gray; head brownish.
Size Length to 21″ (53 cm).
Nesting **Nest:** Large and basket-like, in marsh vegetation above water or on dry ground. Nest materials include a wide variety of dead plants. **Eggs:** Normally 7–12, olive.
Habitat Fresh water areas with abundant vegetation along the edge.
Notes Canvasbacks feed by diving for the succulent roots of various plants found at their "lake resort." They also feed on fishes, tadpoles, leeches, snails and mollusks. This is a diving duck that migrates along the coast and nests at inland sites.

Occasionally a female places one or more eggs in the nest of another pair or even another species. This is probably a survival mechanism. It is safer to let another female incubate one or more of your eggs, in case a predator finds your nest—in other words, not to place all your eggs in one basket.

Observations: ____________, 20____; ____
____

Ring-necked Duck *Aythya collaris*

Description **Male:** Back dark; chest black; head purple, often appearing black. **Female:** Dark brown, white eye ring.
Size Length to 18″ (45 cm).
Nesting **Nest:** On the ground or on floating vegetation. Nest materials include grass, sedges and weeds; nest is lined with down. **Eggs:** Normally 8–10, olive to buff.
Habitat Fresh water marshes. The ring-necked duck is a year-round resident that looks very similar to the lesser scaup (p. 21), which it often accompanies.
Notes This omnivore feeds on grain, pond weeds, water lily bulbs, frogs, crawfish, insects and snails. Individuals gather into flocks by early May to migrate to their breeding grounds inland. Many individuals remain near the coast through the winter months. The ring on this species is so difficult to see that perhaps it should be called ring-billed duck.

Observations: ____________, 20____; ____
____

Greater Scaup *Aythya marila*

Description **Breeding male:** Back gray; chest black; head greenish and glossy. The head is smooth and rounded. **Female:** Brown overall; head dark with a white patch adjacent to the bill and a crescent-shaped spot behind the ear.
Size Length to 18″ (45 cm).
Nesting **Nest:** On the ground, often on an island; in loose colonies. Nest is made from dead plants. **Eggs:** Normally 7–9, olive-buff.
Habitat Primarily salt water and large fresh water bodies.
Notes The greater scaup is a common species that winters and migrates along the coast. It is also found inland on a variety of wetlands, but in reduced numbers. It is an agile diver that can spend up to 60 seconds underwater. Greater scaups nest in Alaska and Yukon.
Similar Species: **Lesser scaup** (see below) is quite similar in appearance and are often mistaken for the greater scaup. Head coloration usually differs but it is not a reliable distinguishing characteristic. The greater scaup is slightly larger, and its head is round compared to the more triangular head of the lesser scaup.

Observations: ____________, 20____; ______________________________
____

Lesser Scaup *Aythya affinis*

Description **Breeding male:** Back gray; chest black; head purple (may also show some green). Head is triangular in shape with a peaked crown. **Female:** Brown overall; head with a white patch adjacent to the bill.
Size Length to 16.5″ (41 cm).
Nesting **Nest:** On the ground, often on a freshwater island, made from dry grass, lined with down. **Eggs:** Normally 9–11, olive-buff.
Habitat Primarily near smaller bodies of fresh water deep enough for diving ducks.
Notes The lesser scaup is a year-round resident that is more common inland than its close relative, the greater scaup (see above). It is a common duck that nests on islands when they are available. Meal selections include such gourmet items as mollusks, worms, fry, crawfish, water insects and larvae. The flight of the lesser scaup is well known for its erratic pattern, with much twisting and turning.

Observations: ____________, 20____; ______________________________
____

Harlequin Duck *Histrionicus histrionicus*

Description **Breeding male:** Striking harlequin-like colors. **Female:** Brown overall; head with three white areas.
Size Length to 16.5″ (41 cm).
Nesting **Nest:** On the ground, often near water, made of grasses and twigs, lined with down. **Eggs:** Normally 5–7, pale buff.
Habitat Along the coast and mountain streams.
Notes Harlequin ducks bounce around like corks in the water. For breeding, they favor areas with the roughest of mountain streams. They sometimes get broken bones while being tossed about, but the bones usually mend. Males accompany females to the breeding grounds but do not assist in raising young; instead they return to the coast. The females return to the coast later with that year's young.
The diet of harlequins changes with the seasons. While on the breeding grounds, they feed on aquatic invertebrates such as the larvae of stoneflies, midges and others. Like American dippers (p. 75), they can walk along the bottoms of streams, feeding underwater for up to half a minute. On the coast, however, they feed on other invertebrates, including snails, small crabs, mussels and fish. In some areas, boating activity on sensitive breeding streams interferes with reproduction and feeding.

Observations: ____________, 20____; ______________________________________
____

Black Scoter *Melanitta americana*

Description **Male:** Body entirely black; bill has yellow knob. **Female:** Brownish overall with gray cheek patches.
Size Length to 20.7″ (53 cm).
Nesting This species does not nest in British Columbia.
Habitat Shallow coastal waters in winter.
Notes The black scoter is the least common scoter found in British Columbia. It feeds primarily on mollusks, most notably mussels and other bivalves. It also eats crustaceans, various marine worms and echinoderms.

This species is present in BC only during winter, near mussel beds in bays, estuaries, harbors and similar sheltered sites where the water is less than 36.3′ (11 m) deep.

Observations: ____________, 20____; ______________________________________
____

Surf Scoter *Melanitta perspicillata*

Description Male: Black overall; head with white patches on forehead and back of head; bill large with orange coloration. **Female:** Brown overall; head with white patches on side of face.
Size Length to 21″ (53 cm).
Nesting Nest: On the ground. Nest is made in a depression and lined with down. **Eggs:** Normally 5–9, buff.
Habitat Saltwater and freshwater areas.
Notes The surf scoter is a sea duck that is commonly seen in large flotillas along the coast, sometimes numbering into the thousands. Like other scoters, this one needs a strong wind in order to take off from the water and fly. In late spring, these birds leave the coastline to fly north and breed. Their diet on the coast consists of mollusks, crustaceans and fish.
Similar Species White-winged scoter (*Melanitta fusca*) is similar in appearance, but it displays a prominent white patch on its wings and lacks the bright orange bill and white patches on the head.

Observations: __________, 20___; ____________________

Common Goldeneye *Bucephala clangula*

Description Breeding male: Back and wings black barred with white; breast white; head dark with greenish sheen and a round white spot on the cheek; eyes golden. **Female:** Brown overall; head dark brown.
Size Length to 20″ (50 cm).
Nesting Nest: In a tree cavity, 5–60′ (1.5–18 m) off the ground. **Eggs:** Normally 7–10, olive green.
Habitat Freshwater and saltwater areas.
Notes Both common and Barrow's goldeneyes (see p. 24) are well known for their swift flight and the whistling sound of the air rushing through their wings. Spring courtship rituals include an elaborate head-bobbing display by the male.

Females are known for their determination to find nesting spots—some have even been known to make their way down chimneys in the search. When nature's accommodation is at a premium, they use nest boxes where available, and two females may deposit their eggs in the same nest.

Observations: __________, 20___; ____________________

Barrow's Goldeneye *Bucephala islandica*

Description Breeding male: Back and wings black barred with white; head dark with a purple sheen and a crescent-shaped spot on the cheek. **Female:** Brown overall.
Size Length to 20″ (50 cm).
Nesting Nest: In a tree cavity, rock crevice or nest box. **Eggs:** Normally 7–10, olive green.
Habitat Freshwater and saltwater areas.
Notes Barrow's goldeneyes nest inland and winter along the coast. Like common goldeneyes (see above), which are close relatives, Barrow's goldeneyes are cavity nesters. The newly hatched young tumble out of the nest and bounce unharmed onto the ground, and the female then leads them to water and watches over them for approximately 56 days. On the coast, this diving duck feasts on a wide variety of delicacies such as mussels, clams, snails and barnacles, which are often found by turning up pebbles in shallow water.

Observations: __________, 20____; ______________________________
____

Bufflehead *Bucephala albeola*

Description Breeding male: Back black; lower body white; head iridescent green with a hint of purple and a white patch on the crown. **Female:** Light brown overall; head dark brown with a white spot.
Size Length to 13.5″ (34 cm).
Nesting Nest: In a tree cavity, 2–50′ (.6–15 m) off the ground. **Eggs:** Normally 8–10, cream colored.
Habitat Freshwater and saltwater areas.
Notes This common species, which gets its name from the puffy appearance of its head, is conspicuously small and never found in large numbers. It commonly migrates along the coast where many individuals winter as well. Pairs of buffleheads remain together for a considerable time and repeatedly return to the same nesting area, near water but away from the coast, where they use the abandoned nests of northern flickers (p. 63). Their diet is varied and includes both fish and fish eggs. The bufflehead has been known to live as long as 13 years.

Observations: __________, 20____; ______________________________
____

Hooded Merganser *Lophodytes cucullatus*

Male displaying.

Description **Male:** Head black; crest features a large white patch; back black. **Female:** Body brown; head with a light brown crest.
Size Length to 18″ (45 cm).
Nesting **Nest:** In a large tree cavity close to water, 10–80′ (3–24 m) off the ground. **Eggs:** Normally 10–12; occasionally to 18, white.
Habitat Woodland ponds and rivers.
Notes The impressive spectacle of the male hooded merganser's crest, raised during courtship, is one of the highlights of spring. (At other times, the crest lies flat on the drake's head.) During the summer months, this bird gathers in smaller numbers, while in the fall, larger groups may congregate. The female carries her young by the neck from the nesting cavity to the water.

This species is also one of the fastest of ducks, with a speed that approaches the "velocity of a bullet," as one observer noted. Hooded mergansers can be found from sea level to elevations of 4,800′ (1,440 m).

Observations: ___________, 20____; ____
____

Common Merganser *Mergus merganser*

Male.

Description **Male:** Head green and lacking a crest; breast white. **Female:** Light brown overall; head rust colored with a crest; breast white; distinct border between rust-colored neck and white breast.
Size Length to 25″ (63 cm).
Nesting **Nest:** Usually near water, in a large tree cavity or rock crevice, or under a tree bank. **Eggs:** Normally 8–11, buff.
Habitat Freshwater and saltwater areas.
Notes Like others in the merganser clan, the common merganser is primarily a fish eater. The toothed bill enables this bird to capture the slipperiest of fish. Flocks of common mergansers are known to work collectively to drive fish into a bay and feast on their prize. They also feed on mussels and various other mollusks. The young of this year-round resident eat heartily, up to an impressive 80% of their body weight per day when they are only 10 days old.

Observations: ___________, 20____; ____
____

Red-breasted Merganser *Mergus serrator*

Description **Breeding male:** Head dark green with a shaggy crest; neck with a white ring; breast rusty. **Female:** Head brown, fading to white breast.
Size Length to 23″ (58 cm).
Nesting **Nest:** Usually on the ground, but also in hollow stumps or burrows. The nest is a slight depression or hollow, lined with down. **Eggs:** Normally 7–10, olive buff.
Habitat Lakes, rivers and coastal bays.
Notes The springtime antics of mergansers are a treat to observe. The elaborate courtship display of the red-breasted merganser begins with the male reaching forward with his neck and raising it so that he can abruptly dunk the front portion of his body underwater while keeping his head above the surface. He then opens his bright red bill and pivots his body in a stiff manner. If several suitors are present to compete, the performance is especially spectacular. Eventually the female chooses a single male, and lays her eggs and incubates them herself. She is responsible for raising the young; as many as 100 young from several broods may be watched over by a single female.

Observations: ____________, 20____; ____
____

I Ring-necked Pheasant *Phasianus colchicus*

Description **Breeding male:** Iridescent bronze body; head dark green with red comb and skin surrounding eye; tail very long and pointed. **Female:** Body brown; tail very long and pointed.
Size Length to 33″ (83 cm).
Nesting **Nest:** On the ground. Nest is a depression lined with grass and similar materials. **Eggs:** Normally 10–12, buff.
Habitat Thickets next to agricultural crops.
Notes In the springtime, the magnificent male ring-necked pheasant crows and beats his wings in order to advertise his presence to other males and his harem of females. During courtship, his comb becomes erect and the bare skin around his eye becomes vivid red. This year-round resident, an introduced species from China, has been brought to North America many times, for purposes of sport hunting. Numbers of the ring-necked pheasant are currently dwindling due to loss of habitat and predation by coyotes.

Observations: ____________, 20____; ____
____

Sooty Grouse *Dendragapus fuliginosus*

Description **Breeding male:** Sooty gray; yellow comb above eye; air sacs on neck are yellow when inflated; tail is black with a gray terminal band. **Female:** Brown overall.
Size Length to 22.5" (57 cm) long.
Nesting **Nest:** On the ground, under shelter such as a log or ledge. Nest materials include twigs, conifer needles and leaves. **Eggs:** Normally 5–10, buff with brown speckles.
Habitat Mixed coniferous forests from sea level to subalpine.
Notes The sooty grouse is a year-round resident of Vancouver Island and the coast range. The springtime hooting of the males can be heard for some distance in forested areas. These "songs" consist of 5–8 distinct hoots which are often difficult to follow as they echo in the woods. Sooty grouse normally call from tree limbs. A closely related species, the dusky grouse (see similar species), also inhabits the coast ranges. Bordering sites like Manning Provincial Park actually have both species present.
Similar Species **Dusky grouse (*Dendragapus obscurus*)** has an all-black tail without a gray band. The air sacs on the neck are reddish purple when inflated. During the breeding season male dusky grouse normally call from the ground.

Observations: ____________, 20____; ______________________________
____

White-tailed Ptarmigan *Lagopus leucura*

Description **Summer:** Brown and white; eye comb red; tail white. **Winter:** Overall white, including tail.
Size Length to 12.5" (31 cm).
Nesting **Nest:** On the ground, made from various plants and other materials, lined with feathers. **Eggs:** Normally 2–8, cinnamon with brown speckles.
Habitat Mountainous regions.
Notes The white-tailed ptarmigan, a member of the grouse clan, is a year-round resident of the mountains. It summers in alpine regions, and migrates over short distances and elevations to its winter range. Its coloration is a remarkably effective camouflage. This species can be found farther south than any other ptarmigan in North America. Buds form an important part of its winter diet. Because ptarmigans live in cold, harsh environments, their toes are feathered to the tips to keep them warm in even the coldest weather.

Observations: ____________, 20____; ______________________________
____

Ruffed Grouse *Bonasa umbellus*

Description **Adult:** Brown speckled with white and black; small crest. **Breeding male:** Neck with black ruff.
Size Length to 17″ (43 cm).
Nesting **Nest:** On the ground, usually next to a log or at the base of a tree, made from leaves and grass, lined with feathers. **Eggs:** Normally 9–12, buff, occasionally with brown speckles.
Habitat Woodlands and forest regions.
Notes The ruffed grouse is well known for its loud drumming in the springtime. As part of his breeding display, the male stands on a log with his ruffs extended, tail fanned and wings trailing. At irregular intervals, the bird beats his wings rapidly through the air to make a drumming sound. This display is a way of announcing his presence to other ruffed grouse in the area and claiming his territory. This year-round resident feeds on the buds, seeds and fruit of a wide range of plants. It is known all over the world for its 10-year cycle: over a 10-year period its population increases rapidly for several years, then plummets, and the cycle repeats. Increases in population are followed by increases in predator numbers, which then reduce the ruffed grouse population to very low numbers. These predators include the red-tailed hawk (see p. 37) and red fox.

Observations: ____________, 20____; ______________________________

I California Quail *Callipepla californica*

Description Back and wings brown; chest blue-gray; one or two teardrop-shaped head plumes; chin patch black.
Size Length to 10″ (25 cm).
Nesting **Nest:** On the ground, near a large rock or log. Nest is a depression lined with grass and dead leaves. **Eggs:** Normally 10–16, white.
Habitat A wide variety of open habitats.
Notes The California quail is an active species, often seen scurrying across roads or open areas. It is a year-round resident that is common in California and has been successfully introduced to several areas in Washington and on Vancouver Island. This bird is known for laying its eggs in the nests of other species, including the ring-necked pheasant (see p. 26).

Observations: ____________, 20____; ______________________________

Common Loon *Gavia immer*

Summer.

Description **Summer:** Head black; neck black with a striped white necklace; back black with rows of white spots. **Winter:** Crown and nape dark gray; throat white with a faint white neck-band fading toward the back.
Size Length to 32″ (80 cm).
Nesting **Nest:** At water's edge, made from various aquatic plants piled in the water. **Eggs:** Normally 2, olive spotted with brown.
Habitat Breeds on freshwater lakes and migrates to the ocean and along the coastline.
Notes The distinctive mournful call of the common loon is often heard near lakes, where it breeds, and occasionally along the coast during its annual migration. The common loon population has been reduced, especially in the southern portion of its range. This species migrates along the Pacific coast and inland as it makes its way to and from its breeding grounds, as far north as Alaska. Loons dive to a depth of 264′ (80 m) and have been clocked at speeds of 75 mph (120 km/h) while flying on migration.
Similar Species: **Pacific loon (*Gavia pacifica*)**, with its gray head and purple neck patch in breeding birds, is a similar species that may be observed while on migration. The similar **Red-throated loon (*Gavia stellata*)** displays a gray head and red neck patch in its breeding plumage. As well, the squarish head of the common loon is noticeably different from the more rounded head of both the Pacific and red-throated loons.

Observations: ____________, 20____; ______________________________
____

Pied-billed Grebe *Podilymbus podiceps*

Description Overall chicken-like body shape with short bill. **Summer:** Brown; throat patch black; eyes dark, each with a white eye ring; bill short and white with a dark black ring. **Winter:** Black ring on bill very faint or non-existent.
Size Length to 13.5″ (34 cm).
Nesting **Nest:** Attached to live aquatic plants, near surface of water; made from decaying vegetation. **Eggs:** Normally 4–7, bluish green.
Habitat Year-round in ponds, lakes and marshes.
Notes The pied-billed grebe is a solitary and secretive species that is famous for its wide array of vocalizations during breeding season in spring. Included in its repertoire is a loud and distinctive *kuk-kuk-kuk cow cow cow cowp cowp cowp*, along with various cooing noises and a gobbling call. It is a small grebe, and amazing in its ability to sink slowly into the water, submerging itself completely or up to its neck.

Observations: ____________, 20____; ______________________________
____

Horned Grebe *Podiceps auritus*

Winter.

Description **Summer:** Neck chestnut; horn-like tufts golden. **Winter:** Gray overall with dark back, nape and head. No "horns" present in winter.
Size Length to 15″ (38 cm).
Nesting **Nest:** In shallow water, made from aquatic vegetation. **Eggs:** Normally 4–6, white to pale green or buff.
Habitat Shallow lakes and ponds in summer; ocean in winter.
Notes This grebe is a solitary species that seldom nests in colonies. It also inhabits Eurasia, where it is called the Slavonian grebe. Males and females share the duties of incubating the eggs. Once hatched, all young grebes have a small triangular patch of skin on the top of their heads. This patch changes to deep red as the chick gets excited, such as when it is begging its parents for food. It is likely a stimulus for the parents to feed their young.

Observations: ____________, 20____; ____
____

Red-necked Grebe *Podiceps grisegena*

Description **Breeding adult:** Throat and cheeks white; foreneck reddish. **Winter:** Throat and foreneck dusky; chinstrap white.
Size Length to 20″ (50 cm).
Nesting **Nest:** Floating nest, made from fresh and decayed vegetation and attached to live plants; solitary or in colonies. **Eggs:** Normally 4–5, bluish white.
Habitat Shallow lakes and wetlands during breeding season; along the coast during spring and fall migrations.
Notes As in all grebes, the legs of the red-necked grebe are positioned far back on the body. This placement is excellent for swimming, but in order to fly, the bird requires a stretch of open water approximately 165′ (50 m) long for takeoff. This limits the areas where the species can nest. The red-necked grebe nests alone or in loose colonies in shallow lakes and similar areas. Courtship practices include the male presenting aquatic vegetation to the female. When the young are still very small, they may be observed catching a ride on a parent's back. Common loons (p. 29) have been known to harass red-necked grebes at both nesting and hunting areas.

Observations: ____________, 20____; ____
____

Western Grebe *Aechmophorus occidentalis*

Description Overall black upper parts and white lower parts; head with distinctive black cap; neck long and narrow.
Size Length to 25″ (63 cm).
Nesting **Nest:** Floating nest, made from fresh and decayed vegetation and attached to live plants; in colonies. **Eggs:** Normally 2–4, pale bluish white.
Habitat Breeds on large lakes, and winters along the Pacific coast.
Notes The western grebe uses its long bill to spear fish, the mainstay of its diet. It is normally a gregarious bird, nesting in groups with up to 90 pairs in a colony. The courtship display is truly spectacular—the birds perform their water ballet by skittering upright along the surface of the water. The ritual is enacted by a mated pair of birds, or two males, or (occasionally) one female accompanied by two males. During the winter months, this species has often been observed on the coast in flocks numbering into the thousands. But populations have declined alarmingly in recent years because of disturbances in nesting areas.

Observations: ____________, 20____; ______________________________________

Pelagic Cormorant *Phalacrocorax pelagicus*

Description **Adult:** Black overall; white patches on flanks. **Breeding adult:** Crown and nape with tufts.
Size Length to 26″ (65 cm).
Nesting **Nest:** On a cliff; in colonies. Nest materials include seaweed, grass, moss and sticks. **Eggs:** Normally 3–5, bluish white.
Habitat Coastal waters.
Notes The pelagic cormorant is the smallest and sleekest of our 3 western cormorant species. An expert fisher, like other ocean-going birds, it removes excess salt from its body through salt glands and excretes the salts in a concentrated solution. It also regurgitates pellets containing the indigestible parts of its prey, much as owls do.
Similar Species **Brandt's cormorant (*Phalacrocorax penicillatus*)** is a similar species, but has a blue and yellow throat, and it seeks out rapidly moving waters. (Pelagic and double-crested cormorants prefer quieter areas.)
Double-crested cormorant (see p. 32), which may also be seen on inland waters, has a yellow-orange throat pouch and is the only west coast cormorant to fly with a kinked neck.

Observations: ____________, 20____; ______________________________________

Double-crested Cormorant *Phalacrocorax auritus*

Description **Adult:** Black overall; throat yellow-orange. **Breeding adult:** Crown with two tufts.
Size Length to 32″ (80 cm).
Nesting **Nest:** On the ground, often on an island or on a man-made structure. Nests in colonies. **Eggs:** Normally 3–4, bluish white.
Habitat Lakes inhabited by fish.
Notes In the world of the double-crested cormorant, the changing of the guard at the nest site is an elaborate and romantic endeavor. The bird that has rested flies to the nest, parades regally around the sitting partner, then tenderly nudges it and eventually places its head under the wing of the sitting bird. The sitting bird then flies off to join other cormorants. This species is a summer resident in areas where there is a good source of fish. After fishing, they often stretch their wings out to dry in the sun, since they do not have natural waterproofing for their feathers. Like members of the owl clan, cormorants regurgitate pellets that contain indigestible materials such as fish bones. Both pelicans and cormorants incubate their eggs in an unusual manner compared with other species. They use their webbed feet, rather than a brood patch (a bare patch of skin on the breast), to cover the eggs and keep them warm.

Observations: ____________, 20____; ______________________________
____

American Bittern *Botaurus lentiginosus*

Description Upper parts rich brown; neck highlighted with a black streak.
Size Length to 28″ (70 cm).
Nesting **Nest:** Above shallow water in thick marsh growth. **Eggs:** Normally 3–5, pale brown to olive-buff.
Habitat Prairie ponds, marshes and similar areas.
Notes The American bittern is well known for its distinctive *onk-a-BLONK* call, which may be heard .6 mile (1 km) away. It is also well known for its habit of "hiding" from intruders by pointing its bill and head skyward and remaining motionless. Its coloration also greatly aids it in staying inconspicuous among the cattails and similar marsh vegetation. The male may mate with two or three females during the breeding season. Like many species that require marshlands, this species is declining in numbers as their habitat is reduced and eliminated.

Observations: ____________, 20____; ______________________________
____

Great Blue Heron *Ardea herodias*

Description Back and wings blue-gray; head white with black bar above eye; legs and neck very long.
Size Length to 46″ (115 cm).
Nesting Nest: In a tree, made from sticks; in colonies. Usually to 20–60′ (6–18 m) off the ground, occasionally more than 100′ (30 m) up. **Eggs:** Normally 3–5, pale blue.
Habitat Freshwater shorelines.
Notes The great blue heron, a striking bird, is commonly seen throughout much of North America. It is an expert fisher that is often observed standing in shallow water, patiently waiting for the right moment to strike. This heron feeds on fish, but also on frogs, salamanders, shrews and voles. If disturbed at a fishing site, it creates a great commotion, uttering a series of prehistoric-sounding shrieks—seemingly in anger at the intruder—before flying off. Herons' courtship rituals include elaborate displays and presentations of sticks. Their colonies are easily disturbed and should not be approached, because great blue herons abandon their nests with little provocation.

Observations: ____________, 20____; ____
____

Green Heron *Butorides virescens*

Description Adult: Upper parts green; back and sides of neck chestnut; legs yellow. **Breeding male:** Legs bright orange. **Juvenile:** Upper parts brownish; underparts heavily streaked with brown.
Size Length to 46″ (115 cm).
Nesting Nest: In a shrub or tree, 5-30′ (1.5–9 m) off the ground. **Eggs:** Normally 3–5, pale green to blue-green.
Habitat Lakes, ponds, marshes and similar areas.
Notes Patience is the key for a hunting green heron, which waits for its prey, silent and motionless, in the water or in overhanging branches of various wetlands. This heron feeds primarily on fish and it is a cunning predator, dropping twigs or other objects on the surface of the water to attract curious fish to the surface, then nabbing them. Like other members of the heron family found here, this species is a summer resident that migrates as far south as Panama and South America.

Observations: ____________, 20____; ____
____

Black-crowned Night-Heron *Nycticorax nycticorax*

Description Back and crown black; gray above, white below; cheek white, head plumes white.
Size Length to 25″ (63 cm).
Nesting **Nest:** On the ground or in a tree, to 150′ (45 m) off the ground. **Eggs:** Normally 3–4, pale green.
Habitat Various marshes.
Notes This chunky-looking species is cosmopolitan in nature, present on every continent except Australia and Antarctica. It is normally a colonial nester. During the day it can be seen sitting motionless in trees near water, but at dusk it begins to forage for food or to fly overhead to reach a nearby food source. The bird's diet includes fish, amphibians, insects, small mammals and the young of a variety of birds found in wetlands. The male is larger than the female, with a deeper voice and a call that is a harsh and guttural wok. At the present time this species is only common at Reifel Migratory Bird Sanctuary in Delta.

Observations: ____________, 20____; ____

Turkey Vulture *Cathartes aura*

Description **Adult:** Brownish black overall; head small, red and unfeathered compared to the bald eagle (see p. 35). **Juvenile:** Head black.
Size Length to 32″ (80 cm).
Nesting **Nest:** In a sheltered location such as a cliff, cave or dense thicket. **Eggs:** Normally 2, placed on ground or on debris, whitish with brown and lavender blotches.
Habitat Primarily observed in flight, or while roosting on open snags.
Notes It is truly amazing to watch turkey vultures as they soar, apparently effortlessly, without so much as a single wing beat. With their V-shaped wings, these masters of the air often ride thermals in the company of bald eagles. They are summer residents, present only during the warmer months of summer. By October, however, turkey vultures begin to migrate south, to South America. The turkey vulture is actually related more closely to the stork family than to the hawk family! This bird has a highly developed sense of smell, with which it finds carrion, its main food item. Turkey vultures perform an important duty as sanitation engineers. They also have an amazing ability to tolerate botulism—an essential feature if you feed on carrion. These birds spend a large part of their days roosting in snags.

Observations: ____________, 20____; ____

Osprey *Pandion haliaetus*

Description Chocolate brown above; white below; wings long and angled backward at the bend; dark line from eye to neck; distinctive black "wrists" visible from below when the bird is in flight.
Size Length to 25" (63 cm).
Nesting **Nest:** On top of a tree or snag. Nest is a platform made of sticks. **Eggs:** Normally 3, cream colored with brown blotches.
Habitat Near the ocean, or lakes with fish.
Notes The osprey is a world citizen, truly cosmopolitan in both temperate and tropical areas of the globe. With its dramatic wingspan to 6′ (1.8 m), the bird hovers above the water while hunting for fish. It is well known for its spectacular dives, often emerging from the water with an impressive fish that even a human would be proud of catching, although some fish are lost to raiding bald eagles (see below). The osprey is well equipped to survive with many useful adaptations. Its oily feathers effectively repel water even after repeated dives. The angular shape of the wings ensures that they are not injured when the bird dives into the water at high speed. The talons are more curved than those of other birds of prey and are enhanced by spiny spicules with which the osprey can grasp slippery fish.

Observations: ____________, 20____; ______________________________________

Bald Eagle *Haliaeetus leucocephalus*

Juvenile.

Description **Adult:** Dark brown overall; head white; tail white. **Juvenile:** Overall dark brown; white feathers appear on the head in the fourth year and proportion of white feathers on the head increases with age.
Size Length 31–37" (78–93 cm).
Nesting **Nest:** On a cliff or in a tree, to 180′ (54 m) or more off the ground. Nest is an accumulation of sticks that is added to over the years. **Eggs:** Normally 2, white.
Habitat Along the coast and near large lakes containing fish.
Notes The bald eagle is a grand species that always commands attention, whether it is sitting in a tree or soaring high in the sky. It is a skillful predator, hunting fish, waterfowl and other birds on the water and remaining ever watchful for the right moment to claim its prize. And it is adept at harassing the osprey (see above), causing it to drop its fish; occasionally the eagle will catch the fish at lightning speed before it touches the water. This large bird of prey can use thermals to circle at amazing heights.

Observations: ____________, 20____; ______________________________________

Northern Harrier *Circus cyaneus*

Description **Male:** Gray-blue above; tail long; rump white; breast white and spotted. **Female:** Similar to male but with brown coloration. **Juvenile:** Similar to female but cinnamon below.
Size Length to 23″ (58 cm).
Nesting **Nest:** Over shallow water or on the ground, in a field or marsh. Nest materials include sticks, grass and weeds. **Eggs:** Normally 4–6, bluish white, sometimes spotted with brown.
Habitat Near wetlands.
Notes Once called the marsh hawk, the northern harrier is a common inhabitant of the marsh. It carries out a seemingly endless search for food, travelling more than 60 miles (100 km) per day in search of food. Occasionally this raptor can be seen stalling in mid-flight when a slight movement is detected, then dropping into the grass to collect a treat such as a vole,young bird, frog or grasshopper. The northern harrier flies slowly and near the ground, except during the breeding display and while on migration. Males are well known for their swooping "skydancing" moves early in the breeding season, maneuvers that consist of vertical climbs and dives directed to prospective mates. Males are often polygamou's, mating with as many as three females. The northern harrier normally nests in wetlands, many of which are now being lost to development.

Observations: ____________, 20____; ________________________________
____

Sharp-shinned Hawk *Accipiter striatus*

Description **Male:** Dark blue above; barred breast; wings rounded; tail long, barred and noticeably squared off. **Female:** Dark brown above.
Size Length 9-13″ (23-33 cm).
Nesting **Nest:** Usually in a conifer, 20–60′ (6–18 m) off the ground. Nest is made from sticks and lined with strips of bark. **Eggs:** Normally 4–5, white with brown blotches.
Habitat Forested areas and woodlands.
Notes Fear reigns among many forest birds when this little resident predator is nearby. The sharp-shinned hawk sits quietly on a perch in a wooded area, waiting for its prey, and then chases small birds, dodging branches as it goes. The similar-sized merlin (see p. 39) does not actively hunt by chasing its prey through trees.

Females are much larger and weigh almost twice as much as males. Their prey also differs significantly: females tend to take birds the size of grosbeaks, while males are often successful with junco-sized birds.

Observations: ____________, 20____; ________________________________
____

Cooper's Hawk *Accipiter cooperii*

Description Similar to sharp-shinned hawk but larger; slate-gray above; tail longer, barred and rounded; head with black cap.
Size Length 14–19" (35–48 cm).
Nesting **Nest:** In a tree, 25–50' (7–15 m) off the ground, made from sticks and lined with bark strips. **Eggs:** Normally 3–5, bluish white with dark markings.
Habitat Forested areas and woodlands.
Notes Closely related to the sharp-shinned hawk (see p. 36), the Cooper's hawk is larger overall with a longer tail. This hawk feeds primarily on birds as big as ducks, and some small mammals. It is often seen sitting out in the open, waiting to attack its prey rather than chasing it. The Cooper's hawk was once among the most common hawks in North America, but its numbers are declining. Some biologists believe that the reduction in populations of small birds may be the prime cause.

Observations: ____________, 20____; ____

Red-tailed Hawk *Buteo jamaicensis*

Description Dark-brown above; upper surface of tail normally brick red; dark belt across the abdomen.
Size Length to 24" (60 cm).
Nesting **Nest:** In a tree, to 120' (36 m) off the ground, made from sticks and lined with fine materials. **Eggs:** Normally 2–3, white with brown blotches.
Habitat Forested areas.
Notes The red-tailed hawk is a common and widespread bird of prey found throughout much of North America. Often observed sitting on a treetop or a telephone pole, this hawk is ever watchful for its next meal. Courtship rituals often include elaborate dives and other aerial acrobatics. The bird emits a distinctive harsh scream, sometimes transcribed as *keeeeer*, while it circles above the ground. Its diet includes mice, voles, ground squirrels, rabbits, small birds, garter snakes and occasionally insects. Like so many other raptors, this species was persecuted for years and now is protected, performing a valuable service by controlling rodents in agricultural areas. The red-tailed hawk is known to live as long as 16 years.

Observations: ____________, 20____; ____

Rough-legged Hawk *Buteo lagopus*

Description Overall mottled brown; tail white with one or more bands.
Size Length to 22″ (55 cm).
Nesting **Nest:** Usually on a ledge. Nest materials include sticks, bones and debris; nest is lined with grasses and twigs. **Eggs:** Normally 3–5, bluish white with brown and violet blotches.
Habitat Open areas while on migration.
Notes Rough-legged hawks are commonly observed while away from their breeding areas across the North American tundra. This species winters from southern British Columbia to central California, so it is commonly seen in the Pacific Northwest between October and March. This is a large hawk, whose numbers fluctuate widely in response to changes in rodent populations. Occasionally it feeds on birds, amphibians and larger insects as well as rodents. To hunt, this hawk may hover over a potential meal or sit and wait on a perch, much like other hawk species.

Observations: ___________, 20____; ______________________________________

____

American Kestrel *Falco sparverius*

Description **Adult:** Back reddish brown; wings bluish; face white with two black stripes; breast buff colored with black spots.
Size Length to 10.5" (26 cm).
Nesting **Nest:** In a tree cavity, 10-30′ (3-9 m) off the ground. **Eggs:** Normally 4-6, pale brown with brown and gray spots.
Habitat Woodland edges, open sites and similar areas.
Notes The American kestrel is North America's smallest falcon. It is well known for its ability to hover while it hunts for its next meal. It feeds on a wide variety of freshly killed foods, including grasshoppers, beetles, shrews, mice and frogs, but rarely birds. This vocal falcon can be recognized by its commonly heard high-pitched call, *killy-killy-killy*. It is a summer resident that migrates to the warmer climates of Central and South America for winter. Specially constructed nest boxes have been found acceptable by this species for nesting and raising a family.

Observations: ___________, 20____; ______________________________________

____

Merlin *Falco columbarius*

Description **Male:** Light blue above; wings long and pointed; tail long with four black bars; breast streaked with brown. **Female:** Similar but brown overall; larger than male.
Size Length to 12" (30 cm).
Nesting **Nest:** In the abandoned nest of a hawk or crow, 10–60' (3–18 m) off the ground. No new nest materials are usually added. **Eggs:** Normally 4–5, whitish with reddish brown markings.
Habitat Forested areas.
Notes The merlin often occupies the abandoned nest of another species, including other raptors or crows, but it is very adaptable and may also take up residence on a cliff ledge or in a tree cavity. It is a falcon that normally hunts alone, but has been reported to hunt cooperatively with other merlins. In urban areas it frequently feeds on house sparrows (p. 89). It is also known for capturing dragonflies for its dinner. It is reputed to be a belligerent raptor that will not tolerate other birds of prey in its vicinity. The female merlin is larger than the male. Size is an important consideration in identifying this species. Formerly called the pigeon hawk, this small falcon is quite vocal, often heard before it is seen with a high-pitched *ki ki ki ki ki ki ki*.

Observations: ___________, 20____; ______________________________

Peregrine Falcon *Falco peregrinus*

Description Black to bluish above; barred below; wings slender; tail long; head with distinctive dark sideburns.
Size Length to 18" (45 cm).
Nesting **Nest:** On a cliff ledge or tall building. No nest is made. **Eggs:** Normally 3–4, reddish brown with dark brown blotches.
Habitat Along rivers, large streams and marine shorelines.
Notes The Peregrine falcon is often observed quietly sitting on a snag watching for an unwary duck or shorebird. It is the fastest bird in the world, capable of reaching estimated speeds of 200 mph (320 km/h) during a stoop (closed-wing dive). With this speed, the peregrine can kill its prey instantly in the sky, and it has also been reported to catch it in mid-air. The Peregrine rarely hunts birds that are sitting on the water; it waits until they take flight, when they are much more vulnerable. This raptor nests early in the season. It selects a cliff ledge or similar spot, protected from the elements, to raise its young. In many cities today, with the help of humans, peregrines nest on high-rise buildings. Thanks to these protected nesting sites and a diet of rock pigeons (see p. 55), Peregrine falcon populations have increased. The Peregrine is known to live as long as 14 years.

Observations: ___________, 20____; ______________________________

Virginia Rail *Rallus limicola*

Description **Adult:** Upper parts dark brown; cheeks gray; breast, foreneck and wings chestnut; bill and legs reddish. **Juvenile:** Darker overall.
Size Length to 9.5″ (24 cm).
Nesting **Nest:** In marsh areas, often near shallow water. Nest is a platform of cattails, reeds and grasses. **Eggs:** Normally 3–5, buff with brown and gray spots.
Habitat Fresh and brackish marshes.
Notes The Virginia rail is a secretive species that is well known for a variety of calls. In fact, it is so secretive that it is heard more often than it is seen.

Included in its repertoire is the frequently heard *kid kid kidick kidick*, as well as a distinctive series of *oink* calls in decreasing volume. Those who are lucky enough to observe this species will see that its long toes are very effective in keeping it on top of the mud, where it often walks. This rail's diet includes a wide variety of invertebrates, including insects, snails and earthworms, as well as an assortment of aquatic insect larvae.

Observations: ____________, 20____; ______________________________

Sora *Porzana carolina*

Description **Adult:** Back and wings brown; face, center of throat and breast black; bill yellow or greenish. **Juvenile:** Darker overall.
Size Length to 8.75" (22 cm).
Nesting **Nest:** Cup-shaped, inches from the water in thick marsh vegetation. **Eggs:** Normally 10–12, buff with brown spots.
Habitat Cattail marshes and similar areas.
Notes The secretive sora is likely to be heard before it is observed. Its distinctive call—*puweee, puweee*—is often repeated during breeding season. Any sudden sound, such as a splash or a rock hitting the ground, can trigger the unique "song" of the sora, which is a descending whinny. If the bird is seen, it may be only for a few moments as it flutters a short distance in the marsh, but it is a proficient flyer, migrating as far south as South America.

Observations: ____________, 20____; ______________________________

American Coot *Fulica americana*

Description **Adult:** Black overall; bill whitish; legs and feet yellow to orange. **Juvenile:** Legs and feet greenish.
Size Length to 15.5″ (39 cm).
Nesting **Nest:** Floating nest, made of dead vegetation. **Eggs:** Normally 6–11, buff with brownish spots.
Habitat Freshwater marshes, ponds and sloughs.
Notes The American coot is a member of the rail family but resembles a duck. It is a year-round resident with breeding pairs found throughout the Pacific Northwest. Many other individuals migrate in spring from southern climates, including California and Mexico. This bird often forms large flocks during migration.

In the springtime, downy young coots are sometimes observed, but they look so different that the observer cannot always determine what species they are. Their colorful bristle-like orange down does not resemble the plumage of an adult. Eventually these downy young molt, and begin to resemble adults. A whitish shield extends from the bill to the forehead. This shield varies greatly in shape from one individual to another and grows larger during the breeding season. The size and shape of the shield seem to play an important part in birds recognizing each other.

Observations: ____________, 20____; ______________________________________
____

Sandhill Crane *Grus canadensis*

Description Gray overall; cap red; legs and neck very long.
Size Length to 41″ (103 cm).
Nesting **Nest:** On a mound rising above water or on dry ground, made from plant material. **Eggs:** Normally 2, olive mottled with gray or brown.
Habitat Marshes, bogs, swamps and meadows.
Notes The sandhill crane is both a migrant and a summer resident. The migratory flights of this bird are memorable: it circles as it gains great heights, often in good voice. The distinctive musical trumpeting calls are easy to identify and can be heard more than a mile away. This crane is well known for its courtship ballet, a series of graceful jumps, which it frequently conducts while on migration. Young sandhill cranes remain with their parents for up to 10 months.

Birding Tip: To differentiate cranes from herons in flight, remember that cranes fly with their necks stretched out while herons hold their necks in an *S* shape.

Observations: ____________, 20____; ______________________________________
____

Black-bellied Plover *Pluvialis squatarola*

Description **Breeding adult:** Head black with white stripe from nape extending to sides of breast; breast black; back mottled in black and white. **Winter:** breast white mottled black.
Size Length to 11.5″ (29 cm).
Nesting **Nest:** On the ground, often a raised hummock or similar site. Nest is a simple scrape in the ground lined with pebbles. **Eggs:** Normally 4, buff to grayish green with dark blotches.
Habitat Mudflats, beaches, marshes and similar areas.
Notes The black-bellied plover is one of several plovers that inhabit North America. It nests in the Arctic, so it is not commonly observed during the summer months. Juveniles remain in more southerly locations for their first summer and do not migrate to the breeding grounds during the first year.

Birding Tip: Plovers can be distinguished from sandpipers in the field by the way they feed. A plover runs along the beach, pauses and tilts its body forward to nab a tasty morsel near the surface. A sandpiper, on the other hand, runs along the beach, stops and furiously probes into the sand or mud for dinner.

Black-bellied plover in fall plumage.

Observations: __________, 20___; ____________________

Semipalmated Plover *Charadrius semipalmatus*

Description Back dark brown; breast white with a single black necklace; legs bright yellow-orange.
Size Length to 7.5″ (19 cm).
Nesting **Nest:** On the ground, often on an island. Nest is a shallow depression in sand or gravel. **Eggs:** Normally 4, olive with brown blotches.
Habitat Saltwater and freshwater sites.
Notes The semipalmated plover is a locally abundant migrant and summer visitor along much of the outer coast. Most breeding occurs in Alaska and northern Canada. This bird frequents a variety of shorelines, including sandy beaches, mud flats and flooded fields, but it prefers the coast. It often calls with a double whistle while in flight. Some individuals migrate long distances, from as far away as South America. "Semipalmated" refers to the partially webbed toes of the bird.

Observations: __________, 20___; ____________________

Killdeer *Charadrius vociferus*

Description Back dark brown; breast white with a double black necklace; rump reddish orange.
Size Length to 10.5″ (26 cm).
Nesting **Nest:** On the ground, in an open area. Nest is a depression, sometimes lined with pebbles, grass or twigs. **Eggs:** Typically 4, buff with black or brown blotches.
Habitat A wide variety of wetlands, open fields, pastures and occasionally the seashore.
Notes The killdeer, a plover, is a year-round resident along the coast and one of the earliest spring migrants to interior habitats. It places its eggs in a depression on bare ground, and both parents incubate the eggs and care for their young. The killdeer is renowned for its "broken wing" behavior to distract possible predators from the nest. When other dangers are present, such as grazing mammals that might step on the nest, the killdeer's defense is much different: it stands over the nest and scolds the intruder in order to drive it away.

Observations: __________, 20____; ______________________________

____

Black Oystercatcher *Haematopus bachmani*

Description Black overall; eyes yellow; bill bright red.
Size Length to 18.5″ (46 cm).
Nesting **Nest:** In a rock depression or on gravel, lined with pebbles and shells. **Eggs:** Normally 2–3, buff with dark scribbles and blotches.
Habitat Rocky coastal areas.
Notes The black oystercatcher is a striking and often vocal year-round resident. It uses its long bill to probe for marine invertebrates such as plate limpets, shield limpets, black Katy chitons, Pacific blue mussels and, yes, oysters. Researchers have determined that it takes the black oystercatcher a mere 10 seconds to remove and devour a limpet, while it takes an average of 130 seconds to open a large Pacific oyster.

Several predators, including the common raven (see p. 68) and northwestern crow (p. 67), are known to steal eggs from the nest of the black oystercatcher. This predation has caused some individuals to re-nest up to 5 times in one season.

Observations: __________, 20____; ______________________________

____

Greater Yellowlegs *Tringa melanoleuca*

Description Back and wings gray to brown; legs yellow; bill about 1.3 times as long as the head, slender and slightly upturned.
Size Length to 14″ (35 cm).
Nesting **Nest:** On the ground, near water, in a swampy wooded area of the north. Nest is made in a depression sparsely lined with grasses. **Eggs:** Normally 4, buff with gray and brown blotches.
Habitat Freshwater and saltwater shores.
Notes The greater yellowlegs is commonly observed while on migration to and from its breeding grounds in the north.
Similar Species Birders find it a challenge to distinguish this bird from a smaller and very similar species, the **lesser yellowlegs** (see below). When the two species are side by side, the size differences are clear. The calls of the two species also differ: the greater yellowlegs' call is *whew-whew-whew*, while that of the lesser is a simple *tu tu*.

Observations: __________, 20____; ______________________________
____

Lesser Yellowlegs *Tringa flavipes*

Description Back and wings gray to brown; legs yellow; bill about the same length as the head, slender and not upturned.
Size Length to 10″ (25 cm) long.
Nesting **Nest:** A depression on the ground, lined with various grasses and leaves. **Eggs:** Normally 4, buff or yellowish to gray with brown speckles and blotches.
Habitat Flooded fields, shallow freshwater ponds, marshes, estuaries and tidal flats.
Notes The lesser yellowlegs is a dainty species that may be found in both sal water and fresh water but favors freshwater habitats. It is normally observed in British Columbia while on migration. It nests in the boreal forests of northern Canada and Alaska and overwinters from southern United States to southern South America. Researchers have observed that the lesser yellowlegs migrates a little later in spring and earlier in fall compared with the greater Yellowlegs.
Similar Species **Greater yellowlegs** (see above)

Observations: __________, 20____; ______________________________
____

Spotted Sandpiper *Actitis macularius*

Description Head and back brown; breast spotted.
Size Length to 7.5″ (19 cm).
Nesting **Nest:** On the ground. Nest is a depression lined with grass and moss. **Eggs:** Normally 4, buff with brown blotches.
Habitat Primarily near fresh water.
Notes The spotted sandpiper is a common summer resident along the shores of lakes, rivers, streams and various types of marshes. Although this species may be observed in small flocks during migration, individuals are often found alone, walking with a distinctive "teetering" motion.

Researchers have found that in some areas, where there is an abundance of males, the female spotted sandpiper lays a clutch of eggs and then leaves it with the male to incubate and raise the young. She then takes up residence with another male and lays a second clutch of eggs for that male to raise. She may repeat the pattern with as many as 5 males before settling down to remain with her "chosen one."

Observations: ____________, 20____; ______________________________________
____

Black Turnstone *Arenaria melanocephala*

Description Head, wings and breast black; bill short, black and wedge-shaped; belly white; legs dark.
Size Length to 9″ (23 cm).
Nesting This species does not nest in British Columbia.
Habitat Rocky coastal edge.
Notes The black turnstone is common along our coastline. The breeding population of the entire world is limited to the coastal region of western Alaska—a very small area for one species! This shorebird feeds on barnacles, limpets and similar organisms by prying them from rocks. It looks for other food by turning over shells, rocks and seaweeds.
Similar Species **Ruddy turnstone (*Arenaria interpres*)** with a head that is black and white and a white breast with black bib. The back is marked with chestnut with black markings.

Observations: ____________, 20____; ______________________________________
____

Long-billed Curlew *Numenius americanus*

Description Overall a rather nondescript, mottled brown color. There is also a pinkish-cinnamon coloration, especially noticeable on the of the spread wing linings. Tip of bill has noticeable curve.
Size Length to 26″ (66 cm) long.
Nesting **Nest:** Placed on the ground normally near a noticeable rock or similar object. Nest is a simple scrape in the ground lined with a few grasses and weeds. **Eggs:** Normally 4, pale buff to olive-buff, with brown and dark olive spots.
Habitat Nests in grasslands but found near various coastal waters on migration
Notes The long-billed curlew is our largest shorebird. Its impressive bill is down-curved and and long, reaching 7″ (18 cm) in length. The male is well known for its amazing displays over nesting territory with an undulating flight that rises higher and flying with an undulating motion, rising higher and finishing with loud ringing calls.
Similar Species **Whimbrel (*Numenius phaeopus*)** is similar but with a shorter bill and a very dark stripe through the eye. It also lacks pinkish cinnamon wing linings.

Observations: __________, 20____; ____________________

Surfbird *Aphriza virgata*

Description **Summer:** Brown spotted with black; capulars rufous; bill short and yellowish; legs greenish yellow. **Winter:** Gray overall; lower breast white.
Size Length to 10″ (25 cm).
Nesting **Nest:** On dry ground. Nest materials include dead leaves and moss. **Eggs:** Normally 4, buff with reddish brown spots.
Habitat Rocky coastal areas.
Notes "Surf's up" in the world of the surfbird. It is often found at the edge of the water, where the surf laps at its feet. This bird is a common winter visitor along the coast and is also observed on migration to its breeding range in the alpine areas of Alaska and the Yukon. This species can often be observed in small flocks in the intertidal zone, feeding on barnacles, limpets, snails, mussels and a variety of other marine organisms. To feed, it uses its thick bill to detach marine creatures from rocks and other hard surfaces.

Observations: __________, 20____; ____________________

Sanderling *Calidris alba*

Description **Summer:** Upper parts reddish brown; underparts white. **Winter:** Pale overall; back gray; belly white.
Size Length to 8″ (20 cm).
Nesting **Nest:** On the ground, in an open area. Nest is a slight depression, often lined with leaves. **Eggs:** Normally 4, olive to brown with a few brown and black spots.
Habitat Primarily sandy beaches.
Notes This common winter resident and migrant nests in the Arctic regions of North America, Europe and Asia. It is a delightful species, probably our palest shorebird, and it can be found on every continent at some time or another during the year. Like many shorebirds, each flock performs an aerial ballet that is not soon forgotten. Sanderlings prefer to feed on hard-packed sand beaches during the ebb or receding tide. They have also been observed feeding at midnight under the light of the moon. Perhaps that is because they are romantics, but it is more likely that a low tide occurred at that time.

Observations: ___________, 20____; ____
____

Western Sandpiper *Calidris mauri*

Description Brown overall; wings rufous at base of the scapulars; head with rufous markings; legs and feet black; bill long, pointed and drooping slightly at tip.
Size Length to 6.5″ (16 cm).
Nesting **Nest:** On the ground, often under a shrub. Nest is a depression lined with sedges, leaves and lichens. **Eggs:** Normally 4, whitish to brown with dark brown blotches.
Habitat Saltwater and freshwater beaches, especially mud flats.
Notes The western sandpiper is the most abundant shorebird along the Pacific Northwest coast. Flocks are often seen in spring and fall, flying in unison. Large volumes of high-energy food are required for the thousands of sandpipers that migrate from Peru to the Arctic and back again each year. Like most sandpipers, this species rests with one leg tucked up, making it look as though every bird in the entire group is one-legged. If disturbed, all the birds often hop on one leg rather than using two legs to move.
Similar Species **Semipalmated sandpiper (*Calidris pusilla*)** is a very similar species. It is paler overall, with a short, blunt bill and just a touch of rufous at base of the scapulars in the spring breeding plumage.

Observations: ___________, 20____; ____
____

Least Sandpiper *Calidris minutilla*

Description Back dark brown; bill short; legs short and yellowish.
Size Length to 6″ (15 cm).
Nesting **Nest:** On the ground, near water. Nest is a depression lined with grass. **Eggs:** Normally 4, buff with brown blotches.
Habitat Saltwater and freshwater beaches.
Notes The least sandpiper is the smallest sandpiper in the world. It is a common species that is found in wetlands throughout the region during migration. The birds typically roost individually or in small groups, and nest from western Alaska to Labrador. At mudflats and sand beaches, they feed on worms, small crustaceans and a variety of insects. The least sandpiper is sometimes called a "peep," a term used for any small sandpiper, especially when its identity is in question.

Observations: ____________, 20____; ______________________________________
____

Pectoral Sandpiper *Calidris melanotos*

Description Back and wings brown; breast with prominent streaking; belly white with a "neat dividing line."
Size Length to 8.75″ (22 cm).
Nesting **Nest:** On the ground, in the Arctic. **Eggs:** Normally 4, whitish to olive.
Habitat Wetlands and similar areas.
Notes The pectoral sandpiper's name originates from an inflatable air sac on the male's chest. This sac is puffed out while he performs a unique flight display during courtship. However, the male does not participate in nesting activities. The female is solely responsible for incubating the eggs and raising the young. This species is commonly observed while on migration to its nesting areas in the Arctic tundra from its wintering areas as far away as southern South America. It often forages in areas of heavier vegetation, where it is difficult to observe.

Observations: ____________, 20____; ______________________________________
____

Dunlin *Calidris alpina*

Description **Summer:** Back reddish; wings brown; belly with large, black patch; bill heavy with a drooping tip. **Winter:** Grayish brown overall.
Size Length to 8.5″ (21 cm).
Nesting **Nest:** On the ground. Nest is a slight depression lined with grass and leaves. **Eggs:** Normally 4, olive with brown blotches, especially at larger end.
Habitat Gravel, sand and mud beaches.
Notes The dunlin is one of the most abundant shorebirds found along the Pacific coast in winter. During its migration to its northern breeding grounds in the Arctic, this species travels in flocks numbering into the tens of thousands. It feeds along a variety of shorelines, and can be found inland on lakes, rivers, sloughs and similar wetlands. The dunlin is also one of the shorebirds renowned for its spectacular group aerial ballets, in which it may be accompanied by the sanderling (see p. 47).

Dunlin on spring migration.

Observations: ___________, 20____; ______________________________

Long-billed Dowitcher *Limnodromus scolopaceus*

Description Bill is very long and straight; white wedge on back. **Breeding:** Breast is a striking brick brown; back is buff with black speckling. **Winter:** Overall gray; breast white; eyebrow is white with a dark eyeline.
Size Length to 11″ (28 cm) long.
Nesting **Nest:** Placed on ground near water. Nest is a simple depression frequently in a wet meadow lined with sedges, grasses. **Eggs:** Normally 4, olive to brown, spotted with brown markings.
Habitat Shallow freshwater wetlands.
Notes Despite its common name, the bill of the long-billed dowitcher is not reliably longer than the the bill of the short-billed dowitcher (see Similar Species). In fact, the bill of the male long-billed dowitcher is the same length as that of the female short-billed dowitcher, so length is not a reliable field characteristic. The voice of the long-billed is often noted as a harsh *keek*, often in a rapid series; the short-billed is likened to a whistle-like *tlu tu tu*, emited in flight. To aid in its feeding this species has sensitive touch-receptors at the tip of the bill.
Similar Species **Short-billed dowitcher (*Limnodromus griseus*)** has a white belly in breeding plumage and favors saltwater habitats.

Observations: ___________, 20____; ______________________________

Wilson's Snipe *Gallinago gallinago*

Description Brown overall; back striped; bill very long and straight.
Size Length to 10.5″ (26 cm).
Nesting **Nest:** On the ground. Nesting materials include leaves, grass and moss. **Eggs:** Normally 4, buff with dark brown blotches.
Habitat Marshlands and grassy meadows.
Notes Wilson's snipe are year-round residents and world citizens. Both males and females are well known for "whinnying" during their rollercoaster courtship display. This distinctive sound is created when air rushes through their stiff outer tail feathers as they dive. The Wilson's snipe is a solitary species that uses its long bill to probe for earthworms, one of its main foods. It also feeds on cutworms, leeches, grasshoppers, beetles, mosquitoes and other insects. The Wilson's snipe is normally very stealthy when not displaying, so it can startle you if you happen to flush one.

Observations: ____________, 20____; ______________________________

Red-necked Phalarope *Phalaropus lobatus*

Description **Summer:** Overall dark; chin white; neck dark gray with bright reddish brown patch on side. **Winter:** Back and wings gray; underparts white; black bar through eye.
Size Length to 7.75″ (19.5 cm).
Nesting **Nest:** On the ground, near water. Nest is a simple scrape. **Eggs:** Normally 4, olive with dark brown blotches.
Habitat Lakes and large wetlands.
Notes Phalaropes are famous for their "spinning" feeding technique. By swimming in tight circles with their lobed toes, they draw up various invertebrates to the water's surface and quickly dine upon them. Phalaropes are also well known for their reversed gender roles. The females are the more brightly colored, and once the eggs are laid, they leave the more subtly colored male to incubate the eggs and brood the young in the Arctic. Phalaropes are also polyandrous: the female mates with several males and lays eggs for each to incubate. The red-necked phalarope is normally observed during its migration to the Arctic from Peru and vice versa.

Observations: ____________, 20____; ______________________________

Pigeon Guillemot *Cepphus columba*

Description **Breeding:** Overall black; wings with white triangular patch; bill long and black. **Winter:** Overall white; back and wings mottled black.
Size Length to 13.5″ (34 cm).
Nesting **Nest:** Among boulders or in a burrow. Nest is a mere scrape in the dirt. Nest sites are often reused for several years. **Eggs:** Normally 1–2, cream colored to greenish with gray or brown blotches.
Habitat Rocky shores and inshore waters.
Notes The pigeon guillemot, which resembles a seabird dressed in a formal tux, is an agile species that dives to 150′ (45 m) below the surface to forage for its food on the sea bottom. It uses its wings primarily to propel itself underwater and uses its feet for both steering and propulsion. Preferred foods include small fish, shrimps, crabs, marine worms and mollusks, as well as small octopus.

Observations: ____________, 20____; ____
____

Bonaparte's Gull *Chroicocephalus philadelphia*

Description **Summer:** White overall; mantle gray; head black; bill black; legs red. **Winter:** Head white with a black spot at the ear.
Size Length to 14″ (35 cm).
Nesting **Nest:** In a coniferous tree, 4–20′ (1–6 m) off the ground. **Eggs:** Normally 3, olive with brown blotches.
Habitat Near fresh water and salt water.
Notes The Bonaparte's gull is commonly seen along the coast during migration in flocks numbering into the hundreds. It is also found inland, but in smaller numbers. The juvenile resembles the winter adult, but has a dark band on the secondary feathers. The bird acquires the black head of its adult plumage in its second year. The diet of this small gull is determined largely by its habitat. Inland birds are mainly insectivorous, while those along the coast feed on small fish, shrimp, marine worms and crustaceans. These dainty gulls are always a delight to watch as they feed at the edge of the water during migration.

Observations: ____________, 20____; ____
____

Heermann's Gull *Larus heermanni*

Description **Breeding:** Back and wings dark; underparts ashy gray; head white; bill red with black tip. **Non-breeding:** Head has brown streaks.
Size Length to 18.7" (48 cm).
Nesting This species does not nest in British Columbia.
Habitat Coastal waters.
Notes The Heermann's gull is a handsome bird, common along our southern coastline during summer and fall. It migrates north as far as BC from its southern breeding area in Baja California, Mexico. This distinctive species appears to prefer stealing food from other bird species rather than foraging on its own, behavior referred to as kleptoparasitism. This gull is most commonly observed along the coast of southwestern Vancouver Island to Victoria.

Observations: ____________, 20____; ______________________________
____

Mew Gull *Larus canus*

Description Back and wings blue-gray; head white and rounded; bill narrow and yellow; eyes dark.
Size Length to 16" (40 cm).
Nesting **Nest:** On the ground near shoreline, or in a tree to 20' (6 m) off the ground. **Eggs:** Normally 3, olive with brown blotches.
Habitat Near fresh water and salt water.
Notes The mew gull is a dainty species that feeds on fish, worms, insects and a variety of other gourmet items. It is noticeably smaller than most gull species observed in the Pacific Northwest, and it is light and buoyant in flight. Although this species is a common migrant and winter visitor, it is not commonly seen during the summer. This gull makes two calls, one that is sometimes described as *kyah kyah*, and another, *meew meew,* which inspired its common name.

Observations: ____________, 20____; ______________________________
____

Ring-billed Gull *Larus delawarensis*

Description **Breeding adult:** White overall with gray mantle; wing tips black; eyes and legs yellow; bill yellow with a black ring near the tip. **Juvenile:** Head and breast streaked with gray.
Size Length to 17.5″ (44 cm).
Nesting **Nest:** On the ground, often on an island, in colonies. Nest is made from grass, weeds and moss. **Eggs:** Normally 2–4, light brown with dark brown blotches.
Habitat Freshwater and saltwater areas, parks and fields.
Notes The ring-billed gull is common in both coastal and interior regions. Some individuals live here all year round, but most migrate to warmer climes during the winter months. Like many gulls, this one prefers to nest on islands, frequently nesting with other species such as the California gull (see below) and herring gull (p. 54). This species was not always as common as it is today; it is a scavenger and the growing amount of human refuse has greatly aided in expanding its numbers. In fact, it is the most abundant gull found in North America.

Observations: ____________, 20____; ____
____

California Gull *Larus californicus*

Description **Breeding adult:** Back and wings blue-gray; wing tips black; bill yellow with red spot on lower bill; legs greenish to yellowish. This combination distinguishes the California gull from other species. **First year immature:** Head and body dark brown; bill pink with black tip; legs pink.
Size Length to 21″ (53 cm).
Nesting **Nest:** On the ground, often on an island, in colonies. Nest is made from grass and weeds, and lined with feathers. **Eggs:** Normally 2–3, buff, olive or brown with dark brown blotches.
Habitat Along the coast, near lakes, on farmlands and in urban centers.
Notes The California gull is an omnivore, feeding on a wide range of items including insects, fish, refuse and the eggs and young of other birds. This species came to the rescue of Mormon settlers in Salt Lake City in 1848, when a plague of grasshoppers threatened their crops. Today it is sometimes seen following the farmer's plow, feeding on insects. The California gull winters along the California and Baja California coast.

Observations: ____________, 20____; ____
____

Herring Gull *Larus argentatus*

Description **Breeding adult:** Body large and white; mantle gray; wing tips black; feet pink; eye yellow; bill yellow with red spot at tip. **Juvenile:** Overall mottled brown; legs and feet pink; bill dark or yellow with black tip.

Size Length to 25″ (63 cm).

Nesting **Nest:** On the ground, in colonies. Nest is made from grasses and seaweed. **Eggs:** Normally 3, buff with brown blotches.

Habitat Saltwater and freshwater areas.

Notes Often described as "mean-looking," this gull is a year-round resident along the coast, and is commonly found throughout much of the Pacific Northwest during the warmer months of the year. A full 4 years are required for the bird to acquire its adult plumage. The herring gull ranges from sea level to 5,528′ (1,660 m) and always nests in colonies near water. It is known to mate occasionally with other gulls, including the glaucous-winged gull (see below). In the 19th century, this gull was hunted for its eggs and feathers.

Similar Species The **Thayer's gull (*Larus thayeri*)** is a similar-looking species often seen along the coast. Its eyes are dark rather than yellow.

Observations: ____________, 20____; ____

____

Glaucous-winged Gull *Larus glaucescens*

Description **Adult:** White overall; mantle gray; wing tips white; feet and legs pink; bill yellow with red spot on lower bill. **Juvenile:** Overall gray-brown, bill black.

Size Length to 27″ (68 cm).

Nesting **Nest:** On the ground or on a cliff or roof, in colonies. **Eggs:** Normally 2–3, olive with brown scribbles and blotches.

Habitat Saltwater and freshwater areas.

Notes The glaucous-winged gull is the most common gull observed along the coast of the Pacific Northwest. The diet of this species varies greatly, from fries at the local fast food outlet to more natural items such as sea stars, which are foraged from the seashore. This gull, an opportunist, also dines on such things as birds' eggs, Pacific blue mussels, sea urchins, barnacles and fish, to name just a few. Glaucous-winged gulls sometimes feed on clams contaminated with PSP or red tide; remarkably, they regurgitate these clams soon after swallowing them. Banding studies have shown this species to live at least 22 years.

Observations: ____________, 20____; ____

____

Caspian Tern *Hydroprogne caspia*

Description White overall; cap solid black; bill heavy and red; legs black.
Size Length to 21″ (53 cm).
Nesting Nest: On the ground, solitary or in colonies. Nest is a scrape with a lining of grasses and seaweed. **Eggs:** Normally 1–3, pale buff with brown or black spots.
Habitat Protected bays along the coast and freshwater bodies with small fish.
Notes The Caspian tern is a large summer visitor that has dramatically expanded its range in recent years. On the west coast, nesting colonies were once found only at sheltered sites in California. Now, large colonies have been established in protected bays along the coast of Washington, and it is expected to become more common in the Pacific Northwest. This bird is North America's largest tern. It has an impressive wingspan of 50″ (1.2 m) and a distinctive loud, raspy, grating *kraaa* call. Individuals live as long as 12 years, occasionally 17 years.

Observations: ____________, 20____; ______________________________

Ⓘ Rock Pigeon *Columba livia*

Description Highly variable; normally back and wings gray; head dark gray; neck iridescent.
Size Length to 12.5″ (31 cm).
Nesting Nest: On a man-made structure. Nest materials include twigs and grass. **Eggs:** Normally 2, white.
Habitat Urban environments.
Notes The rock pigeon, formerly called the rock dove, was introduced by European settlers over a century ago and is now found over much of North America. Members of the pigeon and dove family are unique in that both male and female adult birds can produce a "milk" in their digestive systems and feed it to their young.

This bird played an important role in saving the Peregrine falcon (see p. 39) from extinction. Because the rock dove lives in cities, it was not contaminated with DDT and similar pesticides, as was other prey of the Peregrine falcon. Those Peregrines that nested in high-rise buildings in large cities were able to safely feed on rock pigeons.

Observations: ____________, 20____; ______________________________

Mourning Dove *Zenaida macroura*

Description Body slender; overall brown; underparts pinkish; tail long and pointed.
Size Length to 12″ (30 cm).
Nesting **Nest:** On the ground or in a tree, normally to 40′ (12 m) off the ground. Nest is flimsy and made from sticks. **Eggs:** Normally 2, white.
Habitat Semi-open areas.
Notes The distinctive song of the mourning dove, a sad-sounding cooing: *oowoowoo-woo-woo*, is likely the origin of its common name. This dove feeds on the seeds of grasses and wildflowers. Like all birds that eat seeds, this one regularly swallows grit or small gravel to aid in digestion. In the northern limit of its range, to central BC, the mourning dove raises a single brood per year. In the south, however (across the southern US), an amazing 6 broods may be produced within one year.

Observations: __________, 20____; ______________________________
____

Ⓘ Eurasian Collared-Dove *Streptopelia decaocto*

Description Gray overall; collar black.
Size Length to 12.5″ (32 cm) long.
Nesting **Nest:** In tree or shrub. Flimsy platform nest of sticks and twigs with no other materials added, 6–70′ (1.8–21 m) above ground. **Eggs:** Normally 2, white.
Habitat Suburbs, wood edges, open areas.
Notes The Eurasian collared-dove was accidentally introduced to the Bahamas in 1974. From there it soon spread to Florida and beyond, and the first recorded sighting in British Columbia was at Creston, BC, in 2008. Today the species is widespread in southern BC. Although it only produces 2 eggs per clutch, it is known to attempt up to 9 clutches per year in warmer areas such as Florida. This bird colonizes new areas at an amazing rate, and some consider it a candidate for the world's most prolific breeder! The Eurasian collared-dove feeds its young with a special "milk" that is synthesized in its crop and then regurgitated.
Similar Species **Band-tailed pigeon** (*Patagioenas fasciata*) is a native species that is gray overall with purplish head and breast and neck with white band on the nape.

Observations: __________, 20____; ______________________________
____

Barn Owl *Tyto alba*

Description Male: Light-colored overall; face heart-shaped; eyes dark. **Female:** Darker overall.
Size Length to 16″ (40 cm).
Nesting Nest: In a barn, cave, hollow tree or similar location. No nest is actually made. **Eggs:** Normally 3–8, whitish.
Habitat Chiefly agricultural areas.
Notes Barn owls nest in buildings such as barns, and are also known to nest in large tree cavities and to accept nest boxes constructed especially for them. This species is restricted to areas with mild winters. Its numbers have declined steadily as agricultural land has been given over to development. The bird is an important predator in such areas, feeding on mice and voles. It is most frequently observed at dusk, and its voice has been described as a raspy, hissing screech.

Observations: ____________, 20____; ______________________________

Great Horned Owl *Bubo virginianus*

Description Back and wings dark brown; throat white; ear tufts widely spaced; eyes yellow.
Size Length to 22″ (55 cm).
Nesting Nest: In the abandoned nest of a hawk, eagle or crow, 20–60′ (6–18 m) off the ground, usually with no new nest materials added. **Eggs:** Normally 2–3, whitish.
Habitat Forested areas.
Notes The great horned owl gets its name from the two tufts of feathers on its head. It is a large species and one of the earliest of all nesters, with incubation beginning in late February or early March. A person who ventures too close to an active nest may be attacked by an angry adult, which may draw blood. This owl feeds on a wide variety of mammals, including porcupines and skunks. It is a fearsome, determined hunter that is undeterred by quills and foul smells. Great horned owls hunt by dusk and by night, and smaller owl species also become the hunted.

Observations: ____________, 20____; ______________________________

Northern Pygmy-owl *Glaucidium gnoma*

Description Brown above; crown spotted; underparts streaked; eyes yellow; tail long.
Size Length to 6.75″ (17 cm).
Nesting **Nest:** In a hollow tree, often in an opening made by a woodpecker, 8–25′ (2.5–8 m) off the ground. **Eggs:** Normally 3–4, white.
Habitat Forested areas.
Notes The northern pygmy-owl is often observed sitting on top of a tree while being mobbed by small birds, which gather and fly at the owl in order to chase it away. In fact, that is often the manner in which birders locate this owl. Eventually the mobbing stops and the owl goes back to sleep. This bird is a predator, active at dusk and dawn and feeding principally on small birds. Two eye-like spots or nape spots are found on the back of the head.

Observations: ____________, 20____; ______________________________

Barred Owl *Strix varia*

Description Brown above; facial disk prominent; eyes dark; belly with vertical streaks.
Size Length to 21″ (53 cm).
Nesting **Nest:** In a natural tree hollow, the abandoned nest of a hawk or crow, or a similar location. **Eggs:** Normally 2–3, white.
Habitat Forested areas.
Notes This common year-round resident occurs in forested areas throughout much of eastern North America and is rapidly expanding its range. Its voice is a distinctive sequence of hoots: *who-cooks-for-you, who-cooks-for-you-all*. Juveniles, however, emit a loud and distinctive *psssssst*, which can be heard between June and August. This call aids birders greatly in locating the barred owl. Diet is primarily forest birds and mice, but this owl also eats reptiles, fish and insects. It is one of the easier forest owls to locate because it often hunts during the day.
Similar Species **Spotted owl (*Strix occidentalis*)**, is another dark-eyed species that lives only in old-growth forests. It is a rare species that can be identified by the white spots on the chest and crown.

Observations: ____________, 20____; ______________________________

Short-eared Owl *Asio flammeus*

Description Back and wings brown; face round; tufts present but small and rarely seen; underside heavily streaked, belly buff.
Size Length to 15″ (38 cm).
Nesting **Nest:** On dry ground, often near a marsh. Nest materials include grass and feathers. **Eggs:** Normally 3–11, white.
Habitat Open meadows and wetlands.
Notes The short-eared owl is a year-round resident that nests in open areas. Its flight is irregular and moth-like. The male executes an impressive courtship ritual using his wings to perform a clapping display. During the winter months, as owls seek out suitable hunting areas, accumulations of several owls may occur. Individuals sit on vantage points, patiently waiting for the slightest movement in order to capture their next meal, often in daylight. The owls remain in an area only as long as the food supply holds.

Observations: ____________, 20____; ______________________________
____

Northern Saw-whet Owl *Aegolius acadicus*

Description **Adult:** Brown above; streaked underparts; crown with short stripes; eyes yellow, tail short. **Juvenile:** Overall reddish; large white area between the eyes.
Size Length to 8″ (20 cm).
Nesting **Nest:** In a hollow tree, often in an opening made by a woodpecker, 15–60′ (4.5–18 m) off the ground. **Eggs:** Normally 5–6, white.
Habitat Forested areas.
Notes The northern saw-whet owl is a common owl that easily goes undetected. Its small size and its habit of sleeping during the day in a shrub or tree aid it greatly in being unnoticed. The observer who does happen to see one will find that this owl is one of the few birds that allows a person to get near it.

During winter, the northern saw-whet owl has been known to capture more food than it can eat at one time, then store it in a nearby tree, where it freezes. Later, the owl thaws the food using the warmth of its body.

Observations: ____________, 20____; ______________________________
____

Common Nighthawk *Chordeiles minor*

Description **Male:** Body and wings dark gray with barring; wings pointed with white patch (pronounced in flight); tail with white bar. **Female:** Throat yellow; tail lacking white bar.
Size Length to 9.5″ (24 cm).
Nesting **Nest:** On the ground or on a flat-topped building. No actual nest is built. **Eggs:** Normally 2, buff with brown blotches.
Habitat A wide variety of open areas and rooftops.
Notes The nighthawk is often heard long before it is observed. Its distinctive call has been described as a nasal *peent*. The bird's long, slender wings give it the agility necessary to capture insects in flight, and it has a relatively large mouth to help catch insects on the wing. The nighthawk is a summer resident, and in October it makes its way south to winter hideaways in Mexico and Central America. The numbers of this species are declining in parts of its range, perhaps because of pesticide use or habitat loss.

Observations: __________, 20____; ______________________________

Anna's Hummingbird *Calypte anna*

Description **Male:** Back green; crown and throat iridescent rose red. **Female:** Green overall, with speckling or small spot of red on throat.
Size Length to 3.5″ (9 cm).
Nesting **Nest:** On a tree branch, normally 4–25′ (1.2–7.5 m) above ground. Nest is cup-shaped and is made with spider webs, the down and fibers of plants, and other materials. **Eggs:** Normally 2, white. Female incubates for only 14–19 days.
Habitat Suburban areas, gardens, residential areas with hummingbird feeders.
Notes This handsome species is our only winter resident hummingbird, and it nests here in winter! Those who watch this hummingbird during winter may observe males performing their courtship ritual, an aerial diving display high above a female, accompanied by a distinctive chirp that is louder than its other vocalizations. The dive chirp is actually produced by the vibrating vanes of the bird's distinctive tail feathers, which have narrow tips. During the summer months this species retreats to higher elevations.

Observations: __________, 20____; ______________________________

Rufous Hummingbird *Selasphorus rufus*

Description **Male:** Back reddish brown; tail rufous; throat iridescent reddish orange. **Female:** Tail rufous.
Size Length to 3.75″ (9 cm).
Nesting **Nest:** In a conifer, 3–30′ (1–9 m) off the ground. Nest is made of plant down, moss, lichens and/or other materials, bound together with spider webs. **Eggs:** Normally 2, white.
Habitat Forest edges, mountain meadows and shores of streams.
Notes Arriving with the first blossoms of spring, the rufous hummingbird is a true bundle of energy. The male can be observed performing dive bombs in order to impress a chosen female hidden on a lower branch. This bird's tiny nest holds 2 pea-sized eggs. The young grow quickly and eventually become big enough to fill the nest completely, reshaping it as they reach fledgling size. Like all hummingbirds, this species can fly forward, fly backward and hover. As they fly from one blossom to another, these tiny jewels feed on nectar and small insects. They are strongly attracted to hummingbird feeders that simulate red flowers in the wild. The rufous is also an aggressive species that has little tolerance for other hummingbirds. This is why people often place several nectar feeders in one area to let all hummingbirds feed.

Observations: ____________, 20____; ____
____

Belted Kingfisher *Megaceryle alcyon*

Description **Male:** Overall blue-gray above and whitish below with a blue-gray necklace. **Female:** Lower breast displays an orange band.
Size Length to 14″ (35 cm).
Nesting **Nest:** A burrow in a bank near water, excavated by the belted kingfisher. No nest materials are added. **Eggs:** Normally 6–7, white.
Habitat Freshwater and saltwater areas.
Notes The kingfisher is distinctive for its loud, raucous, rattle-like call. It is an expert fisher, adept at catching a meal by diving into the water and emerging with a small fish. The bird then returns to its favorite perch to beat the fish on a branch, and often to toss it in the air and catch it head first. Like owls, kingfishers cough up pellets containing the indigestible portions of their meals. In addition to fish, they feed on squid, crabs, clams, insects and mice.

Observations: ____________, 20____; ____
____

Red-breasted Sapsucker *Sphyrapicus ruber*

Description Head, nape and breast bright red; back black with spots; wings black with white patch; belly yellow-striped at edges.
Size Length to 8.5″ (21 cm).
Nesting **Nest:** In a tree cavity, 50–60′ (15–18 m) off the ground. **Eggs:** Normally 3–6, white.
Habitat Forest areas.
Notes The sapsucker clan got its name from the birds' dining etiquette of drilling holes in trees, then returning to collect the beads of sap produced at the chisel holes and the insects that have stuck to it. They do not actually suck sap, but they do feed on sap with their specialized tongues. These year-round residents excavate their own nest holes in trees, which provide nesting sites for many other tree-hole-nesting species.

Observations: ____________, 20____; ______________________________________
____

Downy Woodpecker *Picoides pubescens*

Description Wings black with white spots; head black with white stripes; breast and belly white; bill slender and less than half the length of the head; outer tail feathers white with a few black bars. **Male:** Nape with red bar. **Female:** Nape without red bar.
Size Length to 6″ (15 cm).
Nesting **Nest:** Usually in a cavity of a dead tree, 12–30′ (3.5–9 m) off the ground. **Eggs:** Normally 4–5, white.
Habitat Forested areas.
Notes This year-round resident is North America's smallest woodpecker. Its bill is narrower and shorter than that of the similar-looking hairy woodpecker (below). Both male and female help to excavate a nesting cavity, as well as incubate the eggs and feed their young. During the fall and winter, males and females feed in separate territories, and both select dead limbs on which to drum loudly, thus advertising their presence. Diet includes a wide range of insects, especially beetles and ants, and these birds frequent suet feeders during the winter months.

Observations: ____________, 20____; ______________________________________
____

Hairy Woodpecker *Picoides villosus*

Description Wings black with white spots; head black with white stripes; breast and belly white; bill thickened and long—almost 3/4 the length of the head; outer tail feathers white only. **Male:** Nape with red patch. **Female:** Nape without red patch.
Size Length to 9.25″ (23 cm).
Nesting **Nest:** In a tree cavity, 4–60′ (1–18 m) off the ground. **Eggs:** Normally 4, white.
Habitat Woodlands.
Notes This year-round resident is common throughout much of North America. Dinner consists mainly of the larvae of various beetles and other insects that live in the wood of trees. Surprisingly, hairy woodpeckers occasionally also feed on fruit and seeds. The birds keep their mates all year, although separate territories are maintained by the sexes. The female normally initiates courtship activities by drumming on one of several favorite drum trees, a sound that is often heard in the fall and can be very intense at times. Human beings can hear the drumming 2,400′ (720 m) away. The hairy woodpecker's most common vocalization is *jeek, jeek*, often used as a greeting, or it can be described as a hard *peek* (perhaps easier to remember). Courtship flights may be observed: a pair flies duet style, with one bird taking the lead, then the other.

Observations: ____________, 20____; ______________________________
____

Northern Flicker *Colaptes auratus*

Description Back and wings brown barred with black; belly buff, spotted with black; rump white, very noticeable when bird is in flight; bib black. **Male:** Mustache red.
Size Length to 12.5″ (31 cm).
Nesting **Nest:** In a cavity of a dead tree, 6–20′ (1.8–6 m) off the ground. **Eggs:** Normally 5–8, white.
Habitat Moderately open areas.
Notes The northern flicker often forages for snacks on the ground or in ants' nests. In fact, in the bird world it is the champion for eating ants. Scientists determined in at least one study that 45% of all foods consumed by this woodpecker were ants. One individual was found to have more than 5,000 ants in its stomach. Additional food items in the diet includ a wide variety of insects and a large selection of fruits. The northern flicker is important in providing nest sites for the bufflehead (see p. 24) and other hole-nesters, which occupy the accommodations once the flickers have finished with them.

Observations: ____________, 20____; ______________________________
____

Pileated Woodpecker *Dryocopus pileatus*

Description Back and wings black; head black with white stripes and red crest. **Male:** Mustache red.
Size Length to 16.5″ (41 cm).
Nesting Nest: In a cavity of a live or dead tree, 15–80′ (4.5–24 m) off the ground. No nest materials are added.
Eggs: Normally 3–5, white.
Habitat Mature forests. This species requires large trees for nesting.
Notes "Prehistoric" may best describe the appearance of this large, primitive-looking bird. Its loud, powerful voice makes a sound that could be described as *wucka-wucka-wucka*. The pileated woodpecker is also known for its bursts of drumming, which can be heard at long distances. When foraging, this bird leaves an idiosyncratic calling card. It chisels out large, distinctive rectangular holes while it feeds, primarily on ants living in the trunks of trees. Pairs of pileated woodpeckers remain together year-round and often return to the same area to nest for years. The nest is normally, but not always, chosen so that it faces either east or south. This bird is often easily approached.

Observations: ____________, 20____; ______________________________
____

Willow Flycatcher *Empidonax traillii*

Description Upper parts olive-brown; double wing bars; no conspicuous eye ring; throat white; belly yellowish.
Size Length to 5.5″ (14 cm).
Nesting Nest: In a deciduous tree or shrub, 4–15′ (1–4.5 m) off the ground. Nest is made from grass and bark, and lined with plant down. **Eggs:** Normally 3–4, whitish with brown speckles.
Habitat Thickets and similar areas near water; open riparian and disturbed areas.
Notes The willow flycatcher arrives in May from its wintering area in Central and South America, and often goes undetected until the male proclaims his territory with a distinctive *fitz-bew* "song," the best way to identify this flycatcher.

Observations: ____________, 20____; ______________________________
____

Western Wood-Pewee *Contopus sordidulus*

Description Above dark olive brown; wings elongated with 2 gray wing bars. Perches upright with a noticeable hind-crown.
Size Length to 6″ (16 cm) long.
Nesting **Nest:** Placed on a horizontal limb in a tree, 15-40′ (4.5-12 m) above ground. Nest materials include grass, plant fibers, plant down and lichens. **Eggs:** Normally 3, white with brown and violet blotches.
Habitat Open woodlands, forest edge, prefers broadleaf forests near water courses.
Notes The western wood-pewee is a common flycatcher in British Columbia. It migrates from South America where it winters. The "song" of this species is often stated as a rather harsh and nasal *pee-ear*. The surest way to distinguish many flycatchers is by voice and habitat.
Similar Species **Pacific slope flycatcher (*Empidonax difficilis*)** sings *suwheet* and inhabits coniferous forests.
Olive-sided flycatcher (*Contopus cooperi*) is well known for its song *quick-three-beers*, prefers high, open slopes.
Hammond's flycatcher (*Empidonax hammondii*) song normally includes 3 parts *chi-pit, brrrk* and *griip*, as well as a *peep* call, in a habitat that is primarily open forest gaps and edges.

Observations: ____________, 20____; ______________________________
____

Hammond's Flycatcher *Empidonax hammondii*

Description Upper parts dark gray; head gray, large with a slight peak; eye ring white and tear-shaped behind; bill small and dark.
Size Length to 5.5″ (14 cm).
Nesting **Nest:** In a tree. Cup nest placed on horizontal branch, 10–19′ (3–5.7 m) above ground. Materials include plant fibers, grass, strips of bark and lichens. **Eggs:** Normally 3–4, cream colored with light brown spots.
Habitat Mature coniferous and mixed-wood forests.
Notes The Hammond's flycatcher is often the earliest spring Empidonax flycatcher to arrive in British Columbia. It breeds from California to Alaska and winters in Mexico. It is known to live as long as 7 years. Its call is a *peek* or *weep*, and the song is a three-part mix sometimes described as *chi-pit, brrrk* and *grip*, although one part is often dropped.

Observations: ____________, 20____; ______________________________
____

Warbling Vireo *Vireo gilvus*

Description Upper parts gray; eyes dark without "spectacles"; eyebrow prominent and light colored.
Size Length to 5.25" (13.5 cm).
Nesting **Nest:** In a tree. Deep cup nest normally in a deciduous tree, to 30' (9 m) above ground. Nest materials include bark strips, grasses, leaves and plant fibers. **Eggs:** Normally 3–4, white with black or brown speckles.
Habitat Open deciduous or mixed-wood forests.
Notes The warbling vireo is a nondescript gray bird with a whitish eyebrow. It is often identified by its distinctive but variable song, a fast, undulating, cheerful warble that lasts for about 3 seconds and often ends with a single high-pitched note. The oldest warbling vireo on record was a male that was banded, then recaptured more than 13 years later. The warbling vireo is the most common vireo in British Columbia. Its warbling song is cheery and unique. The male's song has been interpreted to say *receiver receiver receiver receipt*!
Similar Species **Red-eyed vireo (*Vireo olivaceus*)** has olive green upper parts a head with gray cap, white eyebrows, a black eye stripe and red eyes.

Observations: ____________, 20____; ____
____

Gray Jay *Perisoreus canadensis*

Description **Adult:** Wings, tail and back dark gray; head white with a black patch at the back; breast white. **Juvenile:** Body dark gray.
Size Length to 11.5" (29 cm).
Nesting **Nest:** In a conifer, 6–28' (2–8.5 m) off the ground. Nest is made from twigs and bark, and lined with feathers and fur. **Eggs:** Normally 3–4, greenish with brown blotches.
Habitat Generally forests at higher elevations.
Notes This friendly member of the jay clan is familiar to all who travel in the backcountry. It was formerly called the Canada jay, as well as the colloquial names whiskey jack, moose bird and camp robber. The gray jay is widespread and a year-round resident. It nests early in subalpine regions, and incubates its eggs while there is still heavy snow. The young are often fledged at about the same time as the snow melts. The gray jay uses its saliva to wrap insects and stick them to branches during the fall and summer, to eat when other food is not abundant.

Observations: ____________, 20____; ____
____

Steller's Jay *Cyanocitta stelleri*

Description Blue overall; crest black.
Size Length to 11.5″ (29 cm).
Nesting **Nest:** In a tree or shrub, 10–30′ (3–9 m) off the ground. Nest materials include twigs, leaves, moss and mud; nest is lined with fine plant materials. **Eggs:** Normally 4, greenish speckled with brown.
Habitat A variety of habitats at lower elevations.
Notes The Steller's jay is a year-round resident with a harsh, distinctive call described as *shaack-shaack-shaack*. This species, the provincial bird of British Columbia, is commonly seen at feeders, bringing a touch of color and much noise. Sometimes it nests near the feeder, a constant food source—occasionally even just outside a window and well within view!
Similar Species The Steller's jay is often mistaken for the **Blue jay (*Cyanocitta cristata*)**, a similar bird that is blue overall with white patches and a blue crest. The blue jay is a rare species in this area.

Observations: __________, 20____; ______________________________
____

Northwestern Crow *Corvus caurinus*

Description Body entirely black; tail fan-shaped; bill stout.
Size Length to 15.6″ (40 cm).
Nesting **Nest:** In a tree. Platform nest in V of forked branch, 10–19′ (3–5.7 m) above ground. Materials include sticks, bark, plant fibers and mud, with lining of grass, animal fur and rootlets. **Eggs:** Normally 4–5, bluish green with brown and gray blotches.
Habitat Mature coniferous and mixed-wood forests.
Notes The Northwestern crow is one of several species that take the initiative to carry hard-shelled mollusks while flying and to drop them from a height onto a hard surface to break the shell and feed on the contents. This smart species is also known as a kleptoparasite—a species that steals food from other animals, including pigeon guillemots (see p. 51).

Observations: __________, 20____; ______________________________
____

Common Raven *Corvus corax*

Description Black overall; bill very thick; throat feathers long and pointed; tail wedge-shaped.
Size Length to 26.5″ (66 cm).
Nesting **Nest:** On a cliff ledge or in a tall tree. Nest is made from sticks and lined with grass, moss and hair. **Eggs:** Normally 4–6, greenish with brown blotches.
Habitat All habitats.
Notes The common raven is a widespread, year-round resident of the Pacific Northwest. Its voice is a hoarse and raspy *kwawk*, compared to that of the American crow, which is more of a *caw*. The raven can also be called the ballet star of the Corvid family (the crow and jay clan). Gliding, soaring, barrel-rolling and diving are all part of ravens' routine, and they seem to enjoy flying. Their courtship rituals, which take place as early as February, also involve aerial antics.

The well-known behaviorist Konrad Lorenz credited the raven as having the "highest mental development" of any species in the bird world. For example, the bird is capable of working alone or in groups to steal food from predator species. One raven may act as a decoy while another grabs the prize. Wild ravens are believed to live as long as 40 years, occasionally even longer.

Observations: ____________, 20____; ____
____

Purple Martin *Progne subis*

Description **Male:** Body dark, glossy purplish blue. **Female & juvenile:** Underparts gray.
Size Length to 8″ (20 cm).
Nesting **Nest:** Commonly in apartment bird houses and single houses over water. **Eggs:** Normally 4–5, white.
Habitat Towns, cities, farms and similar areas.
Notes The purple martin leads an urban lifestyle, easily taking up residence in apartment-style houses constructed by people. This bird is an asset to man because it feeds on a variety of insects including ants, flies, dragonflies and—yes—mosquitoes. To construct a nest box for this welcome species, consult the references on p. 10 and follow the instructions to ensure that the specific nesting requirements are met. Care should also be taken to keep out other species, especially the house sparrow (p. 89) and European starling (p. 78).

Observations: ____________, 20____; ____
____

Tree Swallow *Tachycineta bicolor*

Description Upper parts dark blue to green; rump dark; underparts white.
Size Length to 5.75″ (14.5 cm).
Nesting **Nest:** In a tree cavity, abandoned woodpecker nest or nest box. Nest materials include grass, moss and pine needles; nest is lined with feathers. **Eggs:** Normally 4–7, pale pink to whitish.
Habitat Woodlands near water.
Notes The tree swallow is a tree-hole nester that also adapts to various man-made structures. These pleasant birds feed on an amazing number of insects, including beetles, flies, grasshoppers and dragonflies. Surprisingly, they also feed on berries and seeds when insects are less abundant. The bird lives 2.7 years on average, and the longest living individual on record died at age 8.
Similar Species: The **Violet-green swallow** (see below).

Observations: ____________, 20____; ____
____

Violet-green Swallow *Tachycineta thalassina*

Description Petite body; white below; rump white-sided; wings long, pointed. Tail slightly notched. **Male:** Above glossy, iridescent purple-green; white extends above eye. **Female:** Dull with brown on head & face.
Size Length to 5″ (13 cm) long.
Nesting **Nest:** Inside a cavity such as woodpecker hole, natural tree cavity or other similar site. Nest materials include grass, small twigs, rootlets, and nest is lined with feathers. **Eggs:** Normally 4–6, white.
Habitat Open areas such as woodlands, cities, towns and agricultural lands.
Notes The violet-green swallow is a striking western species that nests in cliff crevices, nest boxes and occasionally in old cliff swallow or barn swallow nests. Placing nest boxes in suitable areas often draws this species and similar cavity nesters into new areas.

This species, like all swallows, forages on the wing, often in flocks with other species of swallows. The male is well known for singing his courtship song in flight, before sunrise (in the dark), replaying it over: and over *tsip tseet tsip*.
Similar Species **Tree swallow** (see above)

Observations: ____________, 20____; ____
____

Cliff Swallow *Petrochelidon pyrrhonota*

Description Rump buffy; tail square; throat dark chestnut and black.
Size Length to 5.5″ (14 cm).
Nesting **Nest:** On a cliff, building or similar site with an overhang. **Eggs:** Normally 4–5, white to pale pink.
Habitat Rivers, farms, semi-open land and similar areas.
Notes The cliff swallow, also known as the legendary swallow of Capistrano, is a colonial nester and the master mud mason of the bird world. To build the distinctive gourd-like nest, swallows gather and apply mud, one billful at a time. At the initial stages of nest building, they commonly hover in order to anchor the nest securely. With their bills they roll the mud into balls, which are then pressed into place. One colony may have as many as hundreds or thousands of nests. In some areas the birds reuse the nests for years.
Similar Species: **Bank swallow (*Riparia riparia*)** displays a brown necklace-like band across its white chest. This species nests in holes in stream banks and similar sites.

Observations: ____________, 20____; ____
____

Barn Swallow *Hirundo rustica*

Description Back and wings dark blue; throat reddish brown; underparts buff; tail deeply forked.
Size Length to 6.75″ (17 cm).
Nesting **Nest:** Usually in a sheltered location, in a man-made structure. Nest is made from mud and grass, and lined with feathers. **Eggs:** Normally 4–5, white with brown speckles.
Habitat In old buildings and similar structures.
Notes The barn swallow is a common summer resident throughout most of the Pacific Northwest, lingering on the breeding grounds longer than other swallows. One may wonder where the barn swallow nested before human beings provided buildings. Archival field notes and other nesting records show that nesting sites included rock caves, rock cliffs and other natural cavities. These sites may once again become important, as the numbers of barn swallows have declined. Long gone are the days when barns were commonplace—farm and other rural buildings are fewer and farther between.

Observations: ____________, 20____; ____
____

Black-capped Chickadee *Poecile atricapillus*

Description Cap and bib black; cheeks white.
Size Length to 5.25″ (13 cm).
Nesting Nest: In a tree cavity or old woodpecker nest, 5–20′ (1.5–6 m) off the ground, or the bird may excavate its own nest cavity. **Eggs:** Normally 6–8, white with reddish brown speckles.
Habitat Deciduous forests.
Notes This year-round resident is familiar to young and old, and often visits bird feeders. During fall and winter, the black-capped chickadee eats seeds and hides many more. Researchers have determined that the bird grows new brain cells—one cell to remember where it hid each seed. The hippocampus of the brain is used for memory, and new cells replace old ones as they are needed. The black-capped chickadee is known to live as long as 12 years. It is also remarkable for its ability to reduce its body temperature at night by 50–54°F (10–12°C) to save energy.

Observations: ____________, 20____; ____

____

Chestnut-backed Chickadee *Poecile rufescens*

Description Cheek patches white; cap black; sides rich chestnut.
Size Length to 4.7″ (12 cm).
Nesting Nest: In a tree cavity. Abandoned woodpecker nest or natural cavity, 2–20′ (0.6–6 m) above ground. Nest materials include hair, fur, feathers, mosses and plant down.
Eggs: Normally 6–7, white with reddish brown speckles predominantly at large end.
Habitat Coniferous, hardwood and mixed-wood forests.
Notes The chestnut-backed chickadee is a locally common species, easy to identify. As its common name suggests, its chestnut back is distinctive. This year-round resident is known for lining its nest with hair and fur from the many mammals that live within its range, including rabbits, coyote, deer and moose. In some areas this material makes up 50 percent of the nest.

Observations: ____________, 20____; ____

____

Bushtit *Psaltriparus minimus*

Description Body gray. **Male:** Crown brown (coastal birds) or ear patch brown (interior birds).
Size Length to 4.5″ (11 cm).
Nesting **Nest:** In a tree or shrub, 8–35′ (2.5–11 m) off the ground, made of tightly woven grass, moss, leaves, rootlets and twigs, lined with hair and feathers. **Eggs:** Normally 5–7, white.
Habitat Open treed areas and shrubby sites.
Notes The bushtit is well known for its distinctive hanging nest, which resembles a wool sock. This architectural marvel can be as long as 10″ (25 cm) and take up to 6 weeks for a pair of birds to build. Some individuals reuse their nests. This bird consumes a great variety of insects as well as fruit and seeds, and is sometimes observed at feeders. The bushtit can be found from southern BC to central Guatemala.

Observations: __________, 20____; ____________________

Red-breasted Nuthatch *Sitta canadensis*

Description Cap black; eye-line black; underparts rufous.
Size Length to 4.5″ (11 cm).
Nesting **Nest:** Excavated in a tree cavity or in an abandoned woodpecker nest, 5–40′ (1.5–12 m) off the ground. Nest materials include grass, moss, bark and feathers. **Eggs:** Normally 5–6, white.
Habitat Mature coniferous and mixed-wood forests.
Notes The red-breasted nuthatch, a year-round resident, frequents feeders containing sunflower seeds and suet, but it normally finds its food while moving head first down a tree trunk. This is an industrious species, which digs out its own cavities or occupies a disused woodpecker nest. The bird may smear the entrance to its nest cavity with sap to discourage insects such as ants from entering the nesting chamber. Included in the repertoire of songs is the nasal territorial song *yna-yna-yna*.

Observations: __________, 20____; ____________________

Brown Creeper *Certhia americana*

Description Upper parts streaked with brown; underparts white.
Size Length to 5.25″ (13 cm).
Nesting **Nest:** Behind tree bark or in a tree cavity, 5–15′ (1.5–4.5 m) off the ground. Nest materials include twigs, bark, moss and leaves; nest is lined with feathers. **Eggs:** Normally 5–6, white speckled with reddish brown.
Habitat Mature forests.
Notes The brown creeper searches for insects and spiders by starting low on a tree trunk and working its way up and onto the branches in a spiral pattern.

During courtship, the male often chases the female, feeding her as she flutters her wings. The female does all the incubating and brooding of the young, but males help feed the young once they have hatched. Both adults and young hide from predators by pressing their well-camouflaged bodies against the bark of trees. Their song begins with two distinctive notes: *sing! sing*!

Observations: ____________, 20____; ______________________________
____

House Wren *Troglodytes aedon*

Description **Adult:** Back and wings dark brown; belly buff; eyebrow faint; tail long.
Size Length to 4.75″ (12 cm).
Nesting **Nest:** In any natural or man-made cavity. Nest materials include twigs, grass, animal fur and feathers. **Eggs:** Normally 6–7, white with reddish brown blotches.
Habitat Open woods, thickets and gardens.
Notes Aptly named, the house wren has a tendency to nest near people's homes, in any available enclosed space such as old woodpecker holes, nest boxes and drainpipes. The male often makes additional dummy nests for the female to choose from. The house sparrow (see p. 89), an introduced species, competes with this native species for nest sites and is believed to be the reason for the decline of the house wren in some areas. The house wren, in turn, is notorious for destroying or removing other birds' eggs. Scientists are uncertain about the reason for this—perhaps they are reducing the competition for food.

Observations: ____________, 20____; ______________________________
____

Pacific Wren *Troglodytes pacificus*

Description Upper parts reddish brown; lower parts buff-brown with prominent barring; tail very short and often held upright.
Size Length to 4″ (10 cm).
Nesting **Nest:** Any natural cavity up to 6′ (1.5 m) off the ground. Nest is made from grass, moss and rootlets, and lined with hair and feathers. **Eggs:** Normally 5–6, white with reddish brown speckles at the large end.
Habitat Forested areas, especially coniferous forests near water.
Notes The winter wren is a wonderfully vociferous addition to our coniferous forests. It is truly a marvelous experience to follow this bird's loud, melodious song and find the source of it—a very tiny bird. Indeed, the winter wren puts every ounce of its body into its song. Its short tail is often held straight up above its back while it sings.

This year-round resident of coastal areas is thought to be polygamous. Males build several nests and sing to attract mates. The female, drawn by the male's song, inspects a nest before choosing her mate and beginning to nest. All wrens respond readily to squeaking (rather than "pishing") sounds made for the purpose of calling them in.

Observations: ____________, 20____; ______________________________________

____

Marsh Wren *Cistothorus palustris*

Description Black triangular patch with white stripes on back; breast white; belly buff; eye-line white and prominent.
Size Length to 5″ (12.5 cm).
Nesting **Nest:** Attached to cattails, bulrushes or other marsh plants. Nest materials include wet grass, cattails and rushes; nest is lined with grass, plant down and feathers. **Eggs:** Normally 4–5, light brown with dark brown blotches.
Habitat Cattail or rush marshes.
Notes The marsh wren is a songster, and it favors singing sites that are hidden from view. Rarely does the male venture far from such locations. Its distinctive song has been described as everything from a gurgling rattle to a rattling chatter. To view the marsh wren is often difficult—sometimes seemingly impossible. The patient viewer is most likely to be rewarded: eventually the male climbs to a position where he can be seen. This wren builds distinctive, sphere-shaped covered nests among cattails and rushes. Males have been known to make as many as 20 dummy nests, possibly to impress females, to mark territory or to distract predators from the real nest. Males are also known to be polygynous, mating with as many as 3 females each. This is more likely to occur in areas with abundant insects, the main food of this species.

Observations: ____________, 20____; ______________________________________

____

American Dipper *Cinclus mexicanus*

Description Gray overall with a stocky build.
Size Length to 6.5″ (16 cm).
Nesting **Nest:** On a rock ledge or among roots on a stream bank, often behind a waterfall. Domed nest is made from mosses, twigs and grass. **Eggs:** Normally 4–5, white.
Habitat Along clear mountain streams.
Notes The American dipper is capable of walking or swimming along the bottoms of fast-moving streams to obtain food. Meals consist primarily of aquatic insect larvae living under stones, as well as insects flying above the water. The water ouzel, as this bird is sometimes called, raises 2 broods per year in parts of its range. It is a year-round resident that often moves down from higher elevations during the winter months, and its continuous push-ups (bobbing) are characteristic.

Observations: ___________, 20____; ______________________________________

Ruby-crowned Kinglet *Regulus calendula*

Description Above greenish gray; eye ring white; wings dark with 2 white wing bars; below pale greenish gray. **Male:** Crown patch red but often not visible. **Female:** Crown patch absent.
Size Length to 4″ (10 cm) long.
Nesting **Nest:** Builds a deep, hanging cup nest below horizontal branch in a tree, 40–90′ (12–27 m) above ground. Nest materials include moss, lichens, bark strips, spider webs, twigs and rootlets. The nest is lined with feathers, plant down and animal hair. **Eggs:** Normally 7–8, white to buff with brown speckles.
Habitat Woodlands, thickets and shrubs. Nests in coniferous forests and muskegs.
Notes The ruby-crowned kinglet is a tiny resident of the area that is found in a wide range of habitats but prefers conifers for nesting. The song of this species is a happy, rolling melody that is very distinctive and hard to forget once identified.
Similar Species **Golden-crowned kinglet (*Regulus satrapa*)** is a tiny resident species with a bright yellow crown bordered in black and no eye ring.. This kinglet is often detected by its high-pitched, thin calls and songs.

Observations: ___________, 20____; ______________________________________

American Robin *Turdus migratorius*

Description Back and wings gray-brown; breast brick red. **Male:** Head black.
Size Length to 10″ (25 cm).
Nesting **Nest:** In a tree, 5–25′ (1.5–8 m) off the ground. Nest materials include grass, twigs and mud. **Eggs:** Normally 4, light blue.
Habitat A wide range of habitats.
Notes For many people, the song of the American robin marks the arrival of spring. This amazing species has adapted well to human environments and often has 3 clutches in one year. It feeds on earthworms, cutworms and various insects, thriving where many other thrushes have not. In the fall, however, its diet changes considerably to a selection of berries and other fruits. The American robin is a common resident throughout North America, and it winters from southern British Columbia southward. Sometimes individuals are caught in unexpected snowstorms and cannot obtain food. At such times they will eat pieces of apple from a feeder, placed there by people wishing to help them out.

Observations: ____________, 20____; ______________________________

____

Swainson's Thrush *Catharus ustulatus*

Description Back and wings uniform brown to reddish brown; eye ring buffy; breast whitish with dark spots.
Size Length to 7″ (18 cm).
Nesting **Nest:** In a tree. Cup nest on branch, 2–10′ (0.6–3 m) above ground. Nest is made of grasses, mosses, bark strips, fine twigs and other materials, and lined with hair and fine grasses. **Eggs:** Normally 3–4, pale blue with brown spots or blotches.
Habitat Coniferous, hardwood and mixed-wood forests, usually near water.
Notes The Swainson's thrush feeds on berries year-round, and also eats insects and spiders. During migration this bird often travels more than 200 miles during an 8-hour period at night, and feeds in the daylight hours. This raises the question: When do they sleep? Researchers believe they take numerous "mini naps," lasting a few seconds each, during the day. In addition, this bird can apparently rest half its brain by sleeping with one eye closed. The other eye remains open and the other half of the brain stays alert to any threats, including predation. The song of the Swainson's thrush is a slow, rising spiral likened to *Oh, Aurelia will-ya, will-ya, will-yeee*, and its call is a sharp *whit*.
Similar Species **Hermit thrush (*Catharus guttatus*)** is similar but with a reddish brown rump.

Observations: ____________, 20____; ______________________________

____

Varied Thrush *Ixoreus naevius*

Description **Male:** Back grayish blue; breast orange with black necklace; eyebrow and wing bars orange. **Female:** Similar to male, back brown and lacking a necklace.
Size Length to 9.5″ (24 cm).
Nesting **Nest:** In a tree, 5–15′ (1.5–4.5 m) off the ground. Nest is made from twigs, moss, leaves, bark and grass. **Eggs:** Normally 3–4, pale blue with light brown speckles.
Habitat Wet coniferous forests.
Notes The varied thrush is known for producing its distinctive sounds of solitude in the woods: a series of long, loud, penetrating notes, each followed by another note about a second later. This is a forest-loving thrush that is often seen stirring up dead leaves while foraging on the ground for food. Its menu changes from a variety of insects in the summer months to seeds and berries in winter. This thrush is normally found at higher elevations, but winter conditions often push them much lower down.

Observations: ____________, 20____; ____
____

Cedar Waxwing *Bombycilla cedrorum*

Description Brown overall; head with crest; wings gray with red (waxy) spots; tail with yellow (waxy) tip; undertail coverts white; belly yellowish.
Size Length to 7.25″ (18 cm).
Nesting **Nest:** In a tree, 6–20′ (1.5–6 m) off the ground. Nest materials include twigs, grass, moss and hair. **Eggs:** Normally 3–5, gray with brown spots.
Habitat Open areas where berries are available.
Notes The cedar waxwing, one of only 3 species of waxwings worldwide, delights in dining primarily on seasonal fruits. Waxwings are frugivores (fruit eaters), enjoying mountain ash, raspberry, rose, bearberry and juniper, among other fruits. These berries contribute the carotenoid pigments the birds need to produce the wax-like secretions on their wings and tail tips.
Similar Species **Bohemian waxwing (*Bombycilla garrulus*)** is similar in coloration. This winter visitor is a larger bird, with white bars and yellow spots on the wings and cinnamon undertail coverts. It often accompanies the cedar waxwing in winter and breeds in the north.

Observations: ____________, 20____; ____
____

I European Starling *Sturnus vulgaris*

Description Adult: Overall black with white spots (feathers are tipped with white). **Breeding adult:** Body iridescent overall, bill yellow.
Size Length to 8.5″ (21 cm).
Nesting Nest: In a cavity. Nest materials include twigs, grass, leaves and feathers. **Eggs:** Normally 4–6, greenish white or bluish white.
Habitat Farmlands, fields and similar situations; urban settings.
Notes The European starling was introduced to North America over a century ago and is now so common throughout most of the continent that it is regarded as a pest. It is a social species, whose flocks number in the thousands during the winter months. Starlings are aggressive, occupying nesting cavities that would otherwise be used by several native species, and occasionally laying their eggs in the nests of other birds. They are also well known for their ability to mimic the songs and calls of other birds.

Observations: ____________, 20____; ______________________________________

Orange-crowned Warbler *Leiothlypis celata*

Description Adult: Upper parts greenish; eyes with slight black bar through middle; breast indistinctly streaked with olive green; bill small; eye rings broken. **Male:** Crown patch orange, but not always visible.
Size Length to 5″ (13 cm).
Nesting Nest: On the ground, occasionally in a short shrub. Open-cup nest. Materials include grasses, leaves, fine twigs and bark strips, with lining of fine grasses and mammal hair. **Eggs:** Normally 4–5, white or creamy with reddish brown speckles.
Habitat Deciduous forests, shrubby areas and thickets.
Notes The orange-crowned warbler is a nondescript warbler with no distinctive field markings. Its orange crown is not often visible. Banding studies show that this bird lives as long as 8 years and 7 months. It often hovers to capture insects and takes nectar from flowers by piercing their bases.

Observations: ____________, 20____; ______________________________________

Townsend's Warbler *Setophaga townsendi*

Description Back greenish; wings gray; face yellow with dark patch, yellow beneath eye; breast yellow; flanks streaked with black. **Male:** Bib black and large. **Female:** Bib reduced, crown and cheek gray.
Size Length to 5″ (13 cm).
Nesting **Nest:** In a tree. Shallow cup nest on horizontal branch of coniferous tree, 7–60′ (2.1–18 m) above ground. Materials include grass, mosses, bark strips and fir twigs, with lining of mosses, feathers and hair. **Eggs:** Normally 4–5, white with brown speckles and blotches.
Habitat Mature coniferous forests.
Notes Townsend's warblers migrate over a longer period in both spring and fall than other warblers. They nest and feed mainly in and around conifers. This species often hybridizes with other warblers, making identification tricky.

Observations: __________, 20____; ______________________________
____

Common Yellowthroat *Geothlypis trichas*

Description **Male:** Mask black with white border; throat and breast bright yellow; upper parts olive green. **Female:** Face does not have mask; throat and breast yellow; upper parts olive green.
Size Length to 5″ (12.5 cm).
Nesting **Nest:** Near the ground on weeds, grasses and shrubs. Nest materials include weeds, grass, sedges, leaves and bark; nest is lined with grass and hair. **Eggs:** Normally 3–5, whitish with brown and black speckles.
Habitat Wetlands.
Notes A visit to a cattail marsh is not complete until the distinctive voice of the common yellowthroat is heard. Its voice is often described as *whitchity, whitchity, whitchity*, or occasionally as *your money, your money, your money*. Its call sounds like a rubber band—*doink*. The common yellowthroat also has a flight song in which the male begins singing on a low shrub, then flies to a height of 25–100′ (8–30 m) in an undulating pattern, from which it swoops down to a new low perch. The song and various notes are only made on the bird's ascent and at the peak of its display; the descent takes place without calls or song. Males are normally monogamous but in at least one instance a male is known to have had two mates. Brown-headed cowbirds (see p. 88) often deposit their eggs in the nests of this host.

Observations: __________, 20____; ______________________________
____

American Yellow Warbler *Setophaga aestiva*

Description **Male:** Body yellow; underside streaked with red; eye dark. **Female:** Body yellow; eye dark.
Size Length to 5″ (12.5 cm).
Nesting **Nest:** In a tree or shrub, 2–60′ (.5–18 m) off the ground. Nest materials include grass and shredded bark; nest is lined with plant down. **Eggs:** Normally 4–5, whitish with brown and gray speckles.
Habitat Deciduous trees or shrubs.
Notes The brilliant colors of the yellow warbler inspire all who see this bird, and its vibrant song is not soon forgotten. It is a lively song, sometimes described as *sweet-sweetsweet summer swee*—but it certainly loses something in the translation. This species is sometimes parasitized by the brown-headed cowbird (see p. 88). When a nest is parasitized, the yellow warbler either deserts the nest or builds a new nest over the old one. One nest contained a total of 6 nests, 5 of which contained cowbird eggs. In some areas of North America, as many as 75% of warblers' nests have been parasitized, but studies in the Pacific Northwest indicate that the rate here is closer to 15%.

Observations: ____________, 20____; ______________________________

Yellow-rumped Warbler *Setophaga coronata*

Description **Male:** Back, wings and head blue; rump, throat and cap yellow. **Female:** Overall duller in color than the male.
Size Length to 5.5″ (14 cm).
Nesting **Nest:** In a tree, 4–50′ (1–15 m) off the ground. Nest materials include bark, twigs and roots; nest is lined with hair and feathers. **Eggs:** Normally 4–5, cream colored with brown and gray speckles.
Habitat Treed areas.
Notes The yellow-rumped warbler is a fine-dining insectivore, enjoying ants, wasps, house flies, crane flies, gnats, true bugs and other insects. This very early migrant is also known to feed on some vegetation. In springtime, migrants announce their arrival from their winter homes in South America. Their beautiful and distinctive warble has been described as *seet-seetseet-seet trrrrr.* These warblers often accompany other species while on migration.

The yellow-rumped warbler can be separated into two groups or subspecies, the "Audubon's warbler" and "myrtle warbler," which were once considered separate species. Breeding males of both species have distinctive plumage. The adult male "Audubon's warbler" displays bright patches of yellow on the crown, throat, side and rump. The adult male "myrtle warbler" displays bright patches of yellow on the crown, side and rump, but has a white throat and eyebrow. Both subspecies can be observed in the Pacific Northwest, but "Audubon's warbler" is more common.

Observations: ____________, 20____; ______________________________

Wilson's Warbler *Cardellina pusilla*

Description Back and wings olive; underparts yellow. **Male:** Cap black; face yellow. **Female:** Cap sometimes blackish; forehead yellowish.

Size Length to 4.75″ (12 cm).

Nesting **Nest:** On the ground or in a shrub or vine, to 3′ (1 m) off the ground. Nest materials include leaves, grass and moss; nest is lined with grass and hair. **Eggs:** Normally 4–6, cream colored with brown markings.

Habitat Moist woods, bogs and thickets.

Notes The Wilson's warbler is a very active species with a habit of twitching its wings and tail while perched. It is a delightful wood warbler and common in moist areas, where it actively pursues a great variety of insects with aerial acrobatics. This bird's song is loud and has been written as *chi chi chi chi chet chet*. Biologists have discovered that populations breeding as far north as Alaska winter in the southern portion of the wintering range, Central America. However, southern breeding populations, such as those in California, winter only as far south as Baja California. It is unknown why this pattern of migration, called leapfrog migration, occurs.

Observations: ____________, 20____; ______________________________________

____

Western Tanager *Piranga ludoviciana*

Description **Breeding male:** Belly yellow; face red; back black. **Female:** Back gray; head greenish yellow; underparts greenish yellow or gray.

Size Length to 7″ (18 cm).

Nesting **Nest:** In a tree, 15–65′ (4.5–20 m) off the ground. Nest is made from twigs, grass and rootlets, and is lined with hair. **Eggs:** Normally 3–5, bluish with brown blotches.

Habitat Conifer forests in summer.

Notes Although the western tanager is a mountain resident, it is often observed in a wide range of other habitats while migrating to its summer residence. The stunning plumage of this bird is memorable. This tanager may also visit feeders to eat fresh fruit, including halved oranges. While nesting, males are often heard singing their robin-like song from a high perch in the forest canopy. The call is distinctive, a quick *prid-a-dit*. The brown-headed cowbird (see p. 88) is known to parasitize the nests of the western tanager with its eggs.

Observations: ____________, 20____; ______________________________________

____

Black-headed Grosbeak *Pheucticus melanocephalus*

Description **Male:** Head black; bill conical; breast and rump orange; wings and tail dark with bold white bars. **Female:** Upperparts brown with white bars; head with brown patch and white stripe above eye, bill conical.
Size Length to 7.8″ (20 cm).
Nesting **Nest:** In a tall shrub or deciduous tree. Open-cup nest 3–25′ (1–7.5 m) above ground. Materials include twigs and pine needles, with lining of fine plant fibers and animal hair. **Eggs:** Normally 3–4, light greenish blue with reddish brown spots.
Habitat Open deciduous and mixed-wood forests.
Notes The black-headed grosbeak builds a large, very loosely constructed nest—so loose that the eggs can often be seen in the nest when viewed from beneath. Some have suggested that this is a way of cooling the eggs; that is unlikely because this species does not nest in areas of extreme heat. Perhaps these birds just don't see the need to overbuild their nest.

Observations: ____________, 20____; ______________________________

Pine Grosbeak *Pinicola enucleator*

Description **Male:** Gray overall; head, back and underparts tipped with pink. **Female and juvenile:** Gray overall; head, rump and underparts orange.
Size Length to 9″ (23 cm).
Nesting **Nest:** In a conifer, 5–15′ (1.5–4.5 m) off the ground. Nest materials include twigs and rootlets; nest is lined with grasses, lichens and moss. **Eggs:** Normally 2–5, green with brown, purple and black speckles.
Habitat Open coniferous woods.
Notes The pine grosbeak is a colorful resident throughout much of the Pacific Northwest. It appears in abundance in some years and not at all in others, perhaps because of variations in weather or food supply. Its diet includes the fruit of crabapples and the seeds of various conifers, and it is occasionally seen at feeding stations. These birds are seed-lovers, especially fond of sunflower seeds—in fact, their presence is often associated with abundant seed crops. They are believed to nest in subalpine forests, but only a few nests have ever been found. During the winter, the birds move to lower elevations.

Male.

Observations: ____________, 20____; ______________________________

Evening Grosbeak *Coccothraustes vespertinus*

Male.

Description **Male:** Belly and rump yellow; head dark with yellow eyebrow; wings black and white; bill massive. **Female:** Tan overall; wings black with white patches.
Size Length to 8″ (20 cm).
Nesting **Nest:** In a tree, 10–100′ (3–30 m) off the ground. Nest is made from twigs, and lined with grasses, moss and pine needles. **Eggs:** Normally 3–4, bluish with brown blotches.
Habitat Mixed and coniferous woods.
Notes The striking colors of the evening grosbeak often cause a great commotion when the birds are viewed for the first time at a feeder. These birds' insatiable appetite for sunflower seeds in winter is truly remarkable. They also feed on the fruit of saskatoon, chokecherry and pin cherry in season, removing the "useless" pulp to get at the seeds inside. This bird can apply a pressure of 110 lbs (50 kg) with its powerful bill to crack the shells of its food. It is a year-round resident that breeds in mixed woods, and often at higher elevations in the mountains as well. Populations of evening grosbeak fluctuate greatly from year to year.

Observations: ____________, 20____; ____
____

Spotted Towhee *Pipilo maculatus*

Description **Male:** Hood black; breast white below with chestnut sides; eyes red. **Female:** Colors subdued.
Size Length to 8.5″ (22 cm).
Nesting **Nest:** On or near the ground. Nest materials include leaves, bark and grasses. **Eggs:** Normally 2–6, cream colored with brown blotches.
Habitat Forest edges and shrubby areas.
Notes The spotted towhee scratches at the ground using both feet at once, to stir up leaves on the ground in search of food. The cheery *chewink* or *chweee* call of this species can often be heard from ground level before the bird is seen. Males can be heard singing with a high trill as they proclaim their territory from tall shrubs. This sparrow-like bird can be found from southern BC to central Guatemala. It was formerly called the rufous-sided towhee, along with a similar species, the Eastern towhee (*Pipilo erythrophthalmus*), which lacks spots.

Observations: ____________, 20____; ____
____

Savannah Sparrow *Passerculus sandwichensis*

Description Eyebrow yellow; breast and sides streaked; back and wings dark brown.
Size Length to 5.5″ (14 cm).
Nesting **Nest:** On the ground, made from grass, lined with fine grass. **Eggs:** Normally 2–6, whitish with brown speckles.
Habitat Open areas, especially grasslands and wetlands.
Notes This widespread resident may be seen and heard singing on top of a shrub or fence post in open country. Here they nest, going largely undetected until the male proclaims his territory. The male's buzzy "song" may be summarized as *tea tea tea teeeeea today*. The savannah sparrow is a common and widespread species that dines on a variety of foods including seeds, beetles and grasshoppers. Males may have more than one mate, and females have been known to lay eggs in other savannah sparrows' nests as well as their own.

Observations: ____________, 20____; ______________________________
____

Song Sparrow *Melospiza melodia*

Description Breast white with dark brown streaks and central spot; eyebrow gray; bill dark.
Size Length to 6″ (15 cm).
Nesting **Nest:** On the ground or in a tree or shrub, to 10′ (3 m) off the ground. Nest materials include weeds, grass, bark strips; nest is lined with grass, rootlets and hair. **Eggs:** Normally 4, whitish with reddish brown blotches.
Habitat Dense shrubby areas.
Notes This sparrow is a very common resident and visitor throughout much of the Pacific Northwest, from the beach to the mountaintops. Its song is rich and varied, beginning with a *sweet, sweet, sweet* and followed by a trill or warble. It has also been said to sing *hip-hip-hooray boys, spring's here*!—an appropriate phrase, since this sparrow begins its nesting activities as early as April in coastal areas. This bird's song is so distinctive that it is embedded in both its common name and its scientific name, melodia ("singing" or "song").

The song sparrow feeds primarily on seeds and insects, which makes it an important factor in the natural control of weed seeds and injurious insects. Adults may nest more than once during the season, and in fact there is one record of a pair successfully raising 4 broods in one season, the last nest also containing 2 eggs of the brown-headed cowbird (p. 88).

Observations: ____________, 20____; ______________________________
____

Fox Sparrow *Passerella iliaca*

Description Head and back dark brown to dark gray; rump and tail reddish; underparts heavily spotted with a large central blotch; yellow lower mandible (bill).
Size Length to 7″ (18 cm).
Nesting **Nest:** On the ground or in a low shrub or tree, made from grass, weeds and moss, lined with grass. **Eggs:** Normally 2–5, greenish blotched with reddish brown.
Habitat Open shrubby and forest areas.
Notes The fox sparrow is often seen scratching its feet along the ground as it forages for seeds, fruits, insects and various other foods. This species is commonly seen throughout the Pacific Northwest during the warmer months, and is a common year-round resident in coastal areas. It can be found from sea level to subalpine elevations. At low elevations, during the winter, it is especially common in blackberry hedgerows.
Similar Species This common species is easily confused with the **Song sparrow** (p. 84). Both species display spotted underparts and a central breast spot. The fox sparrow is dark overall with a yellow lower mandible and lacks facial markings, while the song sparrow is lighter overall with a gray eyebrow and dark bill.

Observations: ___________, 20____; ____

____

Golden-crowned Sparrow *Zonotrichia atricapilla*

Description Breast and cheeks gray and unstreaked; back streaked with black and brown; wings with two white wing bars. **Breeding:** Head with crown that is golden above the black cap. **Non-breeding:** Head with dull yellow stripe on crown and no black cap.
Size Length to 7″ (18 cm).
Nesting **Nest:** On the ground. Bulky cup nest hidden at the base of shrub (various species). Materials include grass, feathers, ferns and leaves, with lining of fine grass or hair. **Eggs:** Normally 3–5, light blue or greenish with reddish brown spots.
Habitat Open shrubby areas and forest edges.
Notes The golden-crowned sparrow is a winter resident in southwestern British Columbia. It nests from Alaska to central BC. This sparrow was well known to late 19th-century Klondike gold rush prospectors, who referred to it as Weary Willie, with a song that sounded to them like *No gold here* or *I'm so tired*.

Observations: ___________, 20____; ____

____

White-crowned Sparrow *Zonotrichia leucophrys*

Description Crown black and white striped; throat gray; wings and back brown.
Size Length to 7″ (18 cm).
Nesting **Nest:** On the ground or in a low shrub, made from grass, twigs, rootlets and bark, and lined with grass, feathers and hair. **Eggs:** Normally 4–5, whitish to greenish with reddish brown speckles.
Habitat Dense shrubby areas.
Notes The spring arrival of the white-crowned sparrow is a welcome sight after the quiet winter months. It is a common year-round resident in the Pacific Northwest, from sea level to alpine elevations. This sparrow feeds on seeds, insects and occasionally fruit and buds. Its song is vibrant and quite variable, and has been written out as *more-wet-wetter-chee-zee* or the undignified *I I I gotta go wee-wee now*. The white-crowned sparrow often nests in close proximity to humans in both urban and rural settings, including urban residential backyards, orchards, clearcut areas and farmlands.

Observations: ____________, 20____; ____
____

Dark-eyed Junco *Junco hyemalis*

Description **"Oregon" form Male:** Back reddish brown; hood black; breast white; outer tail feathers white. **"Oregon" form Female:** Colors drab overall.
Size Length to 6.25″ (16 cm).
Nesting **Nest:** On the ground. Nest built from grass and leaves, lined with fine grass, hair and feathers. **Eggs:** Normally 3–5, whitish with brown and gray markings.
Habitat A wide variety of habitats.
Notes The coloration of the dark-eyed junco varies considerably across North America, where several forms (subspecies) occur. The "Oregon" form, from the West, is darker and was once considered a separate species. Other forms lack the black hood, and in one other form the bird's back is gray. This year-round resident is a regular visitor to bird feeders over the winter months. The cheery presence of the dark-eyed junco is always a welcome sight!

Observations: ____________, 20____; ____
____

Red-winged Blackbird *Agelaius phoeniceus*

Male.

Description Male: Body black; shoulder patches red edged with yellow. **Female:** Brown overall; heavily streaked below.
Size Length to 8.75″ (22 cm).
Nesting Nest: Attached to cattails, bulrushes or willows. Nest materials include grass, reeds and leaves; nest is lined with grasses. **Eggs:** Normally 3–4, greenish with brown blotches.
Habitat Wetlands.
Notes The colorful red-winged blackbird has been declared the most abundant land bird in North America, with winter numbers in the United States alone estimated at an astounding 190 million.

It is a common and colorful resident, often found in the company of the marsh wren (see p. 74) in spring and summer. The red-winged blackbird is a very vocal species, with a repertoire of many "songs," calls and notes, including *conc-a-ree* or *okalee*, as well as *eat my cheeeses*. Its calls include *chuck* and a metallic *kink*.

Observations: __________, 20____; ____________________________
____

Brewer's Blackbird *Euphagus cyanocephalus*

Description Male: Overall black; head with purplish gloss; eyes yellow. **Female:** Overall brown; eyes brown.
Size Length to 9″ (23 cm).
Nesting Nest: On the ground among tall grass, but more often in a tree, 20–40′ (6–12 m) off the ground. **Eggs:** Normally 4–6, gray to greenish gray with brown spots.
Habitat Prairie, fields and similar dry, open areas.
Notes These blackbirds are colony nesters. They are one of a few species known to often clean each other's feathers, removing lice as they go, a process known as allopreening. To invite another bird to preen, the bird buries its bill in its breast feathers, presenting its fluffed out nape. Female Brewer's blackbirds often present themselves in this way to female red-winged blackbirds, for reasons that remain a mystery. This is the only blackbird species whose head moves constantly, with a jerking motion, as it walks.
Similar Species Both sexes of the **Rusty blackbird (*Euphagus carolinus*)** have yellow eyes and lack the iridescent quality of the Brewer's feathers. For habitat, they prefer wet areas to dry ones.

Observations: __________, 20____; ____________________________
____

Brown-headed Cowbird *Molothrus ater*

Description Male: Head dark brown; body metallic black. **Female:** Overall light brown; breast streaked.
Size Length to 7.5″ (19 cm).
Nesting Nest: None; eggs are laid in other species' nests. **Eggs:** Have been known to lay 70 or more in one season, whitish with brown blotches.
Habitat Rangeland, clearcuts, forest edges and other open habitats.
Notes This common species lays its eggs in the nests of other birds. It has developed several adaptations that make it an effective parasite. The female can lay an egg in a host's nest in less than one minute, while a non-parasitic species requires 21 to 104 minutes. As well, the female cowbird lays an average of 40 eggs during one breeding season, while most perching birds lay 4–6 per clutch. Cowbirds' eggs also require less time to hatch than most species. Not all hosts accept this intruder's egg, however. Among the many responses are to eject the egg outright, to abandon the nest altogether or to construct a new nest over the parasitized one. The brown-headed cowbird is known to parasitize 226 species of birds in North America.

Observations: ____________, 20____; ______________________________

House Finch *Haemorhous mexicanus*

Description Male: Cap, back and wings brown; bib, front of head and rump red; undertail coverts and lower breast whitish striped with brown. **Female:** Overall light brown; breast streaked.
Size Length to 6″ (15 cm).
Nesting Nest: In many situations, including in trees and in holes in structures, 12–15′ (3.5–4.5 m) off the ground. Nest is made from grass, twigs, string and feathers. **Eggs:** Normally 4–5, bluish with black and lavender markings.
Habitat Sunny, open, dry areas.
Notes The house finch is a common year-round resident in much of the Pacific Northwest. It enjoys a meal of fresh fruit, such as the native Pacific crabapple (*Malus fusca*), but unfortunately it is also fond of cultivated fruits. This inclination sometimes gets house finches into a wee bit of trouble, especially since they are gregarious and often accumulate in large numbers in the fall.
Similar Species The **Purple finch (*Carpodacus purpureus*)** is a very similar species, but it lacks the brown cap and its undertail coverts are not usually streaked.

Observations: ____________, 20____; ______________________________

American Goldfinch *Spinus tristis*

Summer Male.

Description **Summer male:** Body yellow; cap and tail black; wings black with white bars. **Summer female:** Body yellowish brown; wings black. **Winter male:** Body yellowish brown; head yellowish. **Winter female:** Body yellowish brown; wings black.

Size Length to 5″ (12.5 cm).

Nesting **Nest:** In a tree or shrub. Nest is compact and well made from plant fibers, spider webs and plant down. **Eggs:** Normally 4–6, bluish white, occasionally with brown speckles.

Habitat Weedy areas and open spaces.

Notes The American goldfinch is primarily a seed eater, favoring the seeds of thistle, dandelion and similar plants. It is a striking species, which also feeds on insects during the summer and dines on smaller seeds at feeders. During the courtship display, the male conducts an exaggerated loop flight while singing his *perchicoree* call. The brown-headed cowbird (see p. 88), which lays its eggs in the nests of many other birds in the Pacific Northwest, is discouraged by the American goldfinch. Its grain diet has been found to retard the growth of young cowbirds, making them unable to fledge.

Observations: ____________, 20____; ____

____

(I) House Sparrow *Passer domesticus*

Description **Breeding male:** Crown gray; nape chestnut; bib black. **Female:** Back streaked; eye stripe buff.

Size Length to 6.25″ (15.5 cm).

Nesting **Nest:** In a cavity, in the nest of other birds. Nest materials include grass, weeds and twigs; nest is lined with feathers. **Eggs:** Normally 3–6, whitish with brown and gray blotches.

Habitat Farms, towns and cities.

Notes The house sparrow, or English sparrow as it is often called, is an introduced member of the weaver finch family that is now common throughout most of North America. It finds an occupied cavity to nest in, then removes the eggs, evicts the adults and kills the young of the resident species. The house sparrow dines on a wide range of foods, including insects, spiders, small fruit, weed seeds, grain and crumbs, and it frequents bird feeders as well. Over the past few years, this species has declined in numbers, due to a reduction in available nest sites.

Observations: ____________, 20____; ____

____

Bibliography

BIRDS

Baron, Nancy & John Acorn. 1997. *Birds of Coastal British Columbia*. Lone Pine Publishing, Edmonton, AB

Campbell, R. Wayne et al. 1990–2001. *The Birds of British Columbia*, Volumes 1–4. UBC Press, Vancouver, BC

Dunne, Pete, D. Sibley, & C. Sutton. 1988. *Hawks in Flight: The Flight Identification of North American Migrant Raptors*. Houghton Mifflin Co. Boston, MA

Johnsgard, Paul A. 1988. *North American Owls: Biology and Natural History*. Smithsonian Institution Press, Washington, DC

Kaufman, Kenn. 1996. *Lives of North American Birds*. Houghton Mifflin Co. Boston, MA

Ritchison, Gary. 1999. *Wild Bird Guides: Downy Woodpecker*. Stackpole Books, Mechanicsburg, PA

Wheeler, Brian K. and William S. Clark. 1995. *A Photographic Guide to North American Raptors. Princeton University Press*, Princeton, NJ

FEEDERS, BIRDHOUSES & ATTRACTING BIRDS

Gerhards, Paul. 1999. *Birdhouses & Feeders You Can Make: Complete Plans and Instructions for Bird-Friendly Nesting and Feeding Sites*. Stackpole Books, Mechanicsburg, PA

Laubach, R. & C. M. Laubach, 1998. *Backyard Birdhouse Book: Building Nestboxes and Creating Natural Habitats*. Story Books, Pownal, VT

Merilees, Bill. 2000. *The New Gardening for Wildlife: A Guide for Nature Lovers*. Whitecap Books, Vancouver, BC

Troops, Connie. 1994. *Bluebirds Forever.* Voyageur Press, Inc.. Stillwater, MN

Glossary

accipiter: a forest hawk belonging to the genus Accipiter.
altricial: referring to hatching that occurs at an early stage of the chick's development.
buteo: a hawk belonging to the genus Buteo.
conifer: an evergreen tree that bears needles.
crepuscular: active before dawn and after dusk.
deciduous: trees that lose their leaves annually.
diurnal: active during daylight hours.
insectivore: feeding on insects.
mandible: lower jaw or bill.
nocturnal: active during darkness.
omnivorous: feeding on both animals and plants.
parasitic: referring to a close relationship in which one species benefits at the expense of another.
polyandry: a mating practice in which a female mates with more than one male, but each male mates with only one female.
polygyny: a mating practice in which one male mates with more than one female, but each female mates with only one male.
precocial: referring to hatching that occurs at a late stage of the chick's development.
primary feathers: the elongated feathers on the last segment of the wing.
riparian: pertaining to or along the edge of a river or stream.
scapular: referring to the shoulder area.
speculum: trailing edge of secondary feathers.

Acknowledgments

I would like to thank the many people who assisted with this project.
Mary Schendlinger for her careful editing.
Nancy Wise for her site photography suggestions.
Jim Salt, who generously aided me in photographing several bird species.
The skilled photographers who provided photos. Their names appear below.

Photo Credits

All photos by J. Duane Sept except the following:
Chris Charlesworth: p. 47T.
Perry S. Dicks: p. 30T, p. 40B, p. 57T, p. 58T.
Heather J. E. England: p. 38T.
Michelle Lamberson p. 77T.
Kevin McKinney: p. 36B.
Susan Servos-Sept: p. 95.

Index

About the Author

Duane Sept is a biologist, freelance writer and professional photographer. His biological work has included research on various wildlife species and service as a park naturalist. His award-winning photographs have been published internationally, in displays and in books, magazines and other publications, for clients that include BBC Wildlife, Parks Canada, Nature Canada, National Wildlife Federation and World Wildlife Fund.

Today Duane brings a wealth of information to the public as an author, in much the same way he has inspired thousands of visitors to Canada's parks. His published books include *The Beachcomber's Guide to Seashore Life in the Pacific Northwest* (Harbour Publishing), *Wild Berries of the Northwest: Alaska, Western Canada and the Northwestern United States* (Calypso Publishing) and *Common Mushrooms of the Northwest: Alaska, Western Canada and the Northwestern United States* (Calypso Publishing).